More Easy Walks in Massachusetts

Ashland, Dover, Easton, Foxboro, Framingham,
Holliston, Hopkinton, Mansfield, Medfield, Natick,
Norfolk, Sharon, Sherborn, Walpole, Westborough

Marjorie Turner Hollman

Copyright © 2015 Marjorie Turner Hollman

MarjorieTurner.com

ISBN: 13:978-0-9892043-3-0

Please do not copy or distribute this copyrighted book. Copies are available on Amazon.com or from the publisher

Maps produced using information from the U.S. Geological Survey

Digital icons open sourced from clker.com

More Easy Walks in Massachusetts: Ashland, Dover, Easton, Foxboro, Framingham, Holliston, Hopkinton, Mansfield, Medfield, Natick, Norfolk, Sharon, Sherborn, Walpole, Westborough

1. Non-fiction 2. Sports and Recreation 3. Hiking 4. Biking 5. Family activities 6. Southern New England outdoor activities 7. Second in the series of *Easy Walks in Massachusetts*

MarjorieTurner.com

Bellingham, MA 02019

Dedication

To those who have challenges of any sort getting out of doors, and simply need some support and encouragement to find places that allow them to explore the wonders of nature safely. May this book offer some of the support needed to discover those magical outdoor spots. As someone who has mobility challenges myself, I cherish the ability to get outdoors with assistance. I owe a deep debt of gratitude to those who design, create and maintain trails, many of which I've found to be "Easy Walks." Thank you.

Contents

Preface vii

Introduction ix

    MAP & SYMBOL KEY xiii

Ashland 15

    Ashland Town Forest 17

    Warren Woods 21

Dover 25

    Noanet Woodlands 27

Easton 31

    Borderland State Park 33

    Natural Resources Trust of Easton Sheep Pasture 37

Foxborough 41

    Nature Trail and Cranberry Bog at Patriot Place 43

    Foxborough State Forest 47

Framingham 51

    Callahan State Park 53

    Cowassock Woods 57

Holliston 61

    Holliston Upper Charles Trail 63

    Wenakeening Woods 67

    Adams Street Conservation Area 71

Hopkinton 75

    College Rock 77

    Hopkinton State Park 81

    Lake Whitehall State Park 85

    Waseeka Wildlife Sanctuary 89

    Hopkinton Center Trail 93

Mansfield 95

    Corporal Hardy Conservation Property 97

    WWII Memorial Rail-Trail 101

    Sweet Pond 105

Medfield 107

    Fork Factory Brook 109

    Rocky Woods 113

    Noon Hill 117

    Shattuck Reservation 121

Natick 125

    Broadmoor Wildlife Sanctuary 127

Norfolk 131

    Stony Brook Wildlife Sanctuary 133

Sharon 137

    Moose Hill Wildlife Sanctuary 139

    Moose Hill Farm 143

Sherborn 147

    Rocky Narrows 149

Walpole 153

    Adams Farm 155

    Bird Park 159

    Walpole Town Forest 163

Westborough 167

    Sandra Pond, Bowman Conservation Area 169

    Walkup Reservation 173

    Mill Pond Trails 177

Resources 179

    Author's Note 181

Preface

In the process of getting the word out about my first trails book, *Easy Walks in Massachusetts*, I searched out new trails to share on my Facebook page, "Easy Walks in Massachusetts." Because of the positive response I received through this form of social media, I was spurred to find more trails to share. I soon realized there was a second book in the making. *More Easy Walks in Massachusetts* is the result of nearly a year's worth of field work and sharing on Facebook, and finally, here we are!

On this journey I've gone to new places, made new friends, and learned what really makes an "Easy Walk." It finally dawned on me (later than you might imagine) that all the walks I take are "Easy Walks," that is, they are mostly level, clear paths, with few rocks or roots, not too long, with something of interest along the way.

I am indebted to all my walking buddies and others I've consulted about local trails: I couldn't have written this book without you! Thanks to Ellen Arnold; Mary Beauchamp; Marc Connelly; Sandra Hayden Henry; Vickie Jaquette; Christine Keddy; Seema Kenny; Carolle Lawson; Catherine Mazurowski; Jennifer

PREFACE

Powell; Gretchen Prieve; Sue and Dave Richardson; Anna, Nicole, and David Rogers; Al Sanborn; Marcella Stasa and Bill Taylor; Robert Weidknecht; and especially to my husband, Jon.

I've learned methods of walking in almost any season and under most conditions (except ice!). God bless those friends who have been willing to meet me at 7AM to squeeze in a walk before the summer sun heated up the trails, as well as those of you who bundled up against the winter chill to join me in getting the field work completed so I could share this information in a timely fashion. It's been fun for me; here's hoping it's been as much fun for each of you. Blessings on you all, and happy trails!

Introduction

More Easy Walks in Massachusetts is not an exhaustive list; in fact, it barely scratches the surface of all the trails that exist in the towns included here. It is, however, a guide to nearby places I've grown to love, each of which offer something special while allowing for easy walking. As in the first book of the series, the focus of this publication is on walking trails. Some locations offer opportunities for kayaking and canoeing, many welcome dogs, some permit dogs off leash, some accommodate horseback riding, and some permit mountain biking. Rail-trails welcome walkers, runners, baby strollers, and bikes. A very few places are handicapped accessible and are so noted. The first publication in this series focused on the Blackstone River watershed, with a few towns in the Upper Charles Watershed as well.

This book moves east, away from the Blackstone River Valley to touch on additional towns in the Upper Charles Watershed, the Neponset River Watershed, as well as the Assabet, Concord and Sudbury watersheds. A number of towns are in the MetroWest section of Massachusetts, and many of the properties listed are overseen by large conservation organizations such as Mass

INTRODUCTION

Audubon, The Trustees of Reservations, Sudbury Valley Trustees, and the Massachusetts Division of Conservation and Recreation (DCR). I found trail maps online for most of the trails included in this book.

You'll notice references to the Bay Circuit Trail, a path that travels from the North Shore, around Boston, and on to the South Shore. Portions of the trail follow roads, but the designers of the trail, which has a long, storied history, have sought out conservation properties to link sections of the trail to the extent possible. You'll be able to walk portions of it in the Ashland Town Forest, Rocky Narrows in Sherborn, Noon Hill in Medfield, Adams Farm in Walpole, Moose Hill Wildlife Sanctuary in Sharon and Borderland State Park in Easton.

Many of the trails included in this book are relatively short, 1-2 miles on average, and they are well-maintained. Some are wide enough to allow for families to walk together side by side. Many properties have additional connecting trails for those who are interested in more challenging walks.

Maps

Location maps are provided. These are not trail maps. Download detailed trail maps using search terms indicated in each trail listing.

My hope is to help the reader understand better how to find the trail heads, and in some instances to see how one trail is connected to another, such as College Rock in Hopkinton and Adams Street trails in Holliston, or Cowassuck Woods in

INTRODUCTION

Framingham and the Ashland Town Forest in Ashland. Boundary marks for any of these properties are approximate only. The maps make no assertion or designation of private property boundaries. Observe all notices of private property and respect them!

Words of Caution

Conditions of access and trail conditions may change at any time. Rights of access (parking, trail routes) cannot be guaranteed and you should be sure never to block roads, gates, or access points with cars. "People trails" exist which stray away from known town or accessible properties. Please respect all posted and private property.

Use common sense while outdoors. Wear comfortable, closed-toe shoes to protect your feet. Bring water, preferably in a light backpack to leave your hands free. Hats are helpful. Windbreakers and/or raincoats can make the difference between a fun walk and a miserable time. Dress in layers.

These hikes are all relatively easy. Falls, trip hazards, sliding on wet rocks, and other accidents are still possible.

Learn to recognize poison ivy, which is ubiquitous in the eastern U.S. The hairy roots of poison ivy climb many trees, are sometimes quite large, and are just as noxious as the foliage. Winter is no protection, so use caution. Technu and Zanfel are helpful to fend off the worst effects of this plant.

Ticks are a concern in almost any weather—but especially in spring, and when it has rained. Wearing light-colored clothing

INTRODUCTION

helps in spotting these vectors of disease. Tuck your long pants into your boots or socks to discourage ticks from finding skin to latch onto. "Tick checks" at the end of hikes are good practice.

Fall is hunting season in New England. The Trustees of Reservations presently allows hunting on almost all their properties. Many state parks in Massachusetts allow hunting. Mass Audubon properties never allow hunting. If you're uncertain about the likelihood of hunters being near trails, wear blaze orange clothing items.

If you are hiking alone, let someone know where you are going! Cell phones often have little or no coverage in the woods, especially if you are in a hilly area, so do not depend on them to get help. Avoid taking walks close to dusk. The sun sets quickly in winter, and a dark, unfamiliar trail is a perfect opportunity for injury. Carry a flashlight, or better still, a headlamp in your pack, just in case. Don't treat the outdoors as a place where "carefree" means "careless."

Most important; get outside and have fun!

MAP & SYMBOL KEY

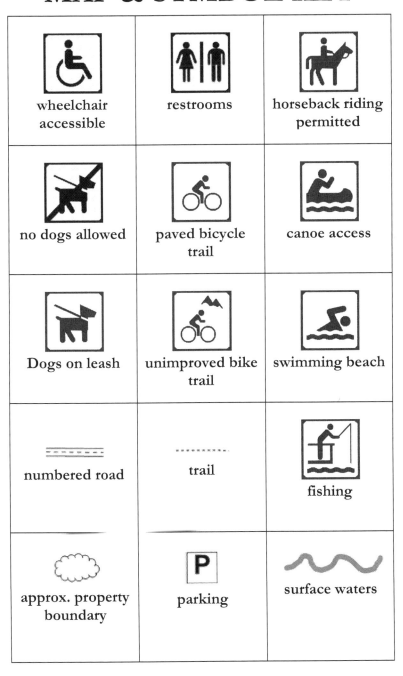

Ashland

ASHLAND

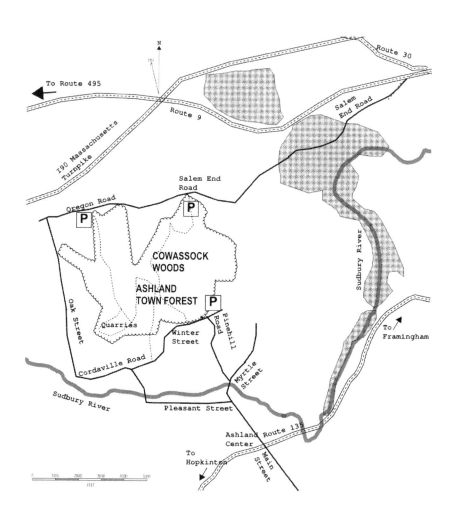

Ashland Town Forest

<u>Features.</u> Adjacent to Cowassuck Woods, in Framingham, Bay Circuit trail traverses property. Small quarries visible from trail.

<u>Trail Map:</u> Online Search—Ashland MA Open Space committee

<u>GPS Coordinates</u>: 42°16'17.53"N 71°28'.19.40"W

ASHLAND

<u>Directions:</u> On Rt. 135 westbound from Framingham to Ashland Center, turn right onto Main Street, 0.5 miles, bear right onto Myrtle Street, cross over the Sudbury River, take the immediate left onto Pine Hill Road. At intersection with Winter Street, turn left onto Winter Street, look for trail kiosk and small parking area on right.

<u>Cost:</u> Free.

<u>Bathrooms:</u> No.

<u>Best time to visit:</u> Year-round.

<u>Trail conditions:</u> Unimproved, clear, wide, smooth, walkable dirt track with few rocks, a few bridges over streams. Some wet spots.

<u>Distance:</u> Loop trail to quarries and back to Winter Street is about 2.5 miles, additional trail distances marked in online map. 500+ acre parcel.

<u>Parking:</u> Small pull-off area next to trail kiosk on Winter Street. Parking is not plowed in winter, but there is room to park on street.

This trail provided one of the most pleasurable walks I found in the course of researching this book. A true "Easy Walk," the trails were wide, smooth, and mostly level. Many trails require watching one's step, walking carefully between rocks and roots, but this trail allowed for steady, easy strides, and we were able to keep up a comfortable pace throughout almost the entire walk, barring the crossing of a very few small streams, when care was needed to keep our feet dry.

There are few parking spaces on Winter Street. Additional parking access is on Oregon Road at the north side of the forest, and from Cowassuck Woods, just over the line in Framingham on Salem End Road, which is a continuation of Oregon Road.

A trail kiosk marks the trail head, which is visible from Winter Street. Blazes mark the trail clearly, and are easy to follow, except in the area near the small quarries which are visible from the trail. In that area we found ourselves off the trail but were able to find our way back with little difficulty. The Bay Circuit Trail travels through this section of forest where the quarries are.

We found many stone walls throughout the property. Printing out an online map is helpful since the area is rather large and there are several trail junctions. The choice of paths can make one's walk much longer than intended.

ASHLAND

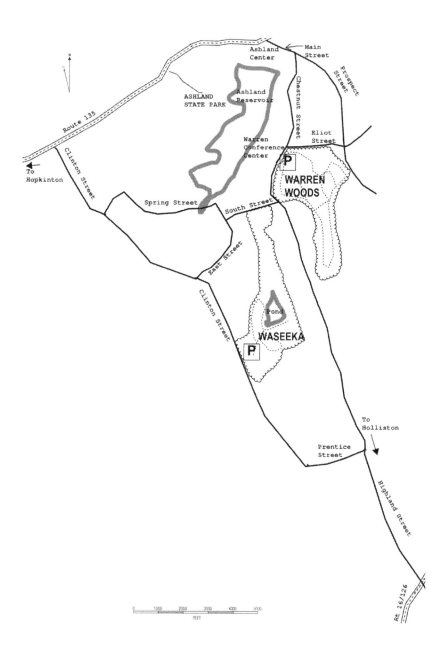

Warren Woods

Features: Stone walls, small streams, old orchards on property. Former farm of Henry Warren (inventor of the electric clock, among other inventions).

Trail Map: Online Search—Ashland MA Open Space committee

GPS Coordinates: 42°14'13.39"N 71°27'28.97"W

ASHLAND

Directions: 529 Chestnut Street, Ashland (address of Warren Center, across the street from Warren Woods). Eastbound leaving Hopkinton on Rt. 135 toward Ashland Center, turn right onto Main Street, travel 0.5 mile, fork to right onto Chestnut Street, continue on Chestnut less than a mile, Warren Conference Center is on right, Warren Woods is across the street on left, small utility building and parking on left. From Holliston center on Rt. 126/16, head west toward Milford, turn right onto Highland Street, follow Highland 3.5 miles to Warren Woods. Highland becomes Chestnut Street, Warren Center on left, Warren Woods on right.

Cost: Free.

Bathrooms: Not available, but portable toilets generally available at sports field across the street.

Best time to visit: Year round, but may be muddy in spring.

Trail Conditions: Narrow unimproved dirt track, some roots and rocks, some wet spots. Only gentle slopes, nothing steep. Trail markings somewhat confusing.

Distance: 142 acres, easy loop trails of about a mile.

Parking: Large parking area next to utility building can be accessed directly from Chestnut Street.

This property was donated by the Henry Warren estate to Northeastern University, and was recently acquired as open space overseen by the Town of Ashland. The property is actually in both

Ashland and Holliston and was purchased using Community Preservation (CPA) funds.

The open fields of this property front onto Chestnut Street in Ashland and offer great views of the Warren Conference Center, directly across the street from the property. Despite the proximity to the busy road, the woods buffer the noise of traffic.

It is easy to picture the land as it was when cultivated—stone walls follow the paths we walked, down a slope to a stream, creating a small dam. Two abandoned orchards on the property are reminders of the area's agricultural past. Kiosks at the trailhead and at the edge of the orchard offer historical information about the property and its former owner, Henry Warren.

Dover

DOVER

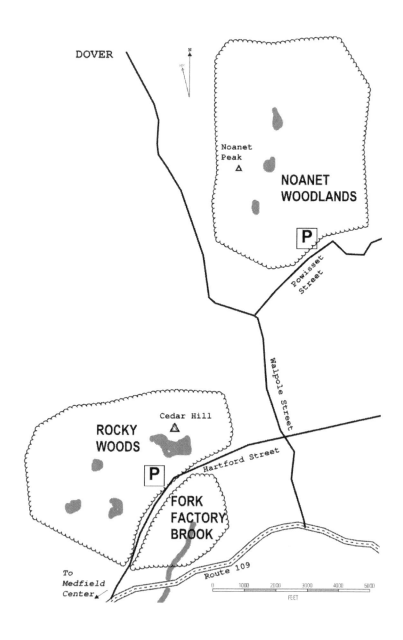

Noanet Woodlands

Features: Views of Boston skyline from Noanet Peak. Large mill pond, stone foundations of mill, 24 ft. high dam.

Trail Map: Online search—The Trustees of Reservations

GPS Coordinates: 42°13'41.71"N 71°15'23.57"W

DOVER

<u>Directions</u>: Rt. 109 and Rt. 27 in Medfield, drive east toward Westwood 2 miles. Turn left onto Hartford Street. Drive 1.5 miles, then turn left onto Walpole Street for 0.8 miles to Powisset Street. Drive 0.6 miles, parking lot is on left.

<u>Cost</u>: Free to all, donations welcome.

<u>Bathrooms</u>: Portable toilets hidden behind wooden screen at parking lot.

<u>Best time to visit</u>: Year round, lot is plowed in winter.

<u>Trail conditions</u>: Unimproved, clear, walkable dirt track, varied terrain, rocky and steep to reach Noanet Peak.

<u>Distance</u>: 17 miles of trails, many shorter loops available.

<u>Parking</u>: 15 cars parking area directly off Powisset Street.

South Central Massachusetts lacks the mountains that lie north of here, and has no ocean views. What it does have is a multitude of mostly level trails to enjoy. There are a few locations with amazing views, and Noanet Peak is one of these places.

The views of Boston and beyond are worth the challenge of tackling the more difficult terrain that immediately surrounds the peak. Once there, enjoy a 170° view. We found the approach to the peak from the north to be easier, while descending the peak trail to the south was quite challenging and rather steep. Noanet Woodlands has an extensive system of networked trails that connect with Rocky Woods, another Trustees property, as well as the Hale Reservation in Westwood (not included in this book).

The mill dam is impressive, with an information kiosk that describes construction of the dam and how the mill wheel functioned. The mill pond next to the dam is quite scenic.

The blue-dot trail was easy walking throughout this property. For easy walking with few challenges along the trail, simply enjoy the mill pond and the stone work around that area and forgo the climb to Noanet Peak.

The Trustees of Reservations allows dogs off leash on this property, but dogs must be under voice control. We found this to be a very popular spot for dog walkers.

Easton

EASTON

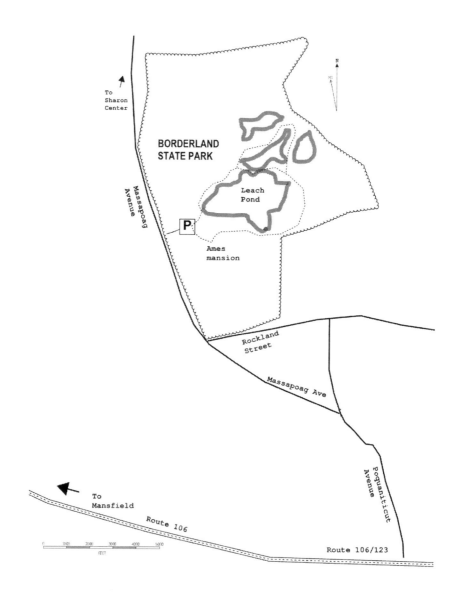

Borderland State Park

Features: Carriage road around several ponds. Bay Circuit Trail traverses this property. Large stone mansion and grounds. Numerous community activities ongoing.

Trail Map: Online search—Borderland State Park

GPS Coordinates: 42°03'38.26"N 71°09'58.66"W

EASTON

<u>Directions</u>: 259 Massapoag Avenue, North Easton, MA. (main entrance) In Mansfield, Rt. 495 to Rt. 140 north for 1.25 miles to Rt. 106, turn right, travel east on Rt. 106 for almost 5 miles. 0.5 miles after Rts. 106 and 123 merge, look for brown "Borderlands" sign at Poquanticut Avenue on left, turn left, travel 1 mile to fork, bear left to Massapoag Avenue, 2 miles to signs for park, on left.

From 95 south: exit 10, Coney Street, Walpole/Sharon, turn left onto Coney Street to lights at Sharon Center (2-3 miles). Go through intersection, immediately bear right onto Pond Street 1.5 miles to rotary; halfway around rotary, turn onto Massapoag Avenue, continue 3 miles to park entrance, on left.

<u>Cost</u>: $5 for parking.

<u>Bathrooms</u>: Available at ranger station when open, daily 8am-4pm during winter; spring-fall, 8am-8pm.

<u>Best time to visit</u>: Year round, parking lots plowed in winter.

<u>Trail conditions</u>: Carriage road is wide, mostly level, hard-packed gravel, easy walking. Grounds around mansion are grassy, additional trails are unimproved dirt track, well-maintained. Trails to the north and west of the large ponds are challenging.

<u>Distance</u>: 20 miles of hiking trails, many shorter loop trails available.

<u>Parking</u>: Multiple parking spaces available, automated system requires dollar bills, post receipt on car dashboard.

Borderland State Park, Easton, MA is a hidden jewel in the DCR state park system. The Ames' stone mansion, surrounded by terraced gardens and a large open field, is impressive both in its size and appearance, clearly visible from the main parking lot across the large open field.

There are multiple trails to choose from in this substantial state park. An attractive carriage path follows the shoreline of two large ponds on this 1000+ acre property. The Bay Circuit Trail follows a portion of the carriage path, quite near the Ames mansion.

At the edge of the pond closest to the visitor's center is a small stone building, perhaps used as a warming hut for skaters when the Ames family was in residence. A disc golf course is laid out in the park; and we saw several disc golf enthusiasts when we visited in the summer. Many community classes and other events are offered at the park throughout the year.

.

EASTON

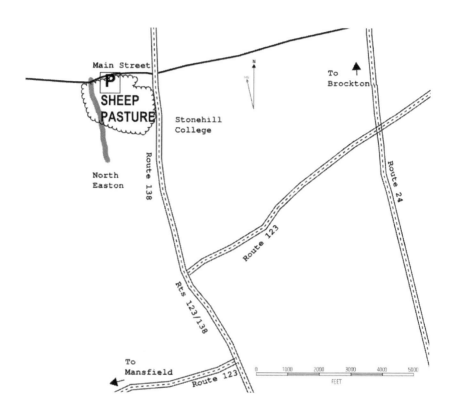

Natural Resources Trust of Easton Sheep Pasture

Features: Trails designed by Frederick Law Olmsted, farm animals, beautiful stand of rhododendrons, which bloom in early June.

Trail Map: Online search—Natural Resources Trust Sheep Pasture/About us/trail map

EASTON

GPS Coordinates: 42°03'59.83"N 71°05'18.18"W

Directions: 307 Main Street, North Easton. From Rt. 495 take exit 10, Rt. 123 East/Norton almost 8 miles, turn left onto Rt. 138 north for about 1.5 miles, pass Stonehill College on right, turn left onto Main Street, first entrance to Sheep Pasture on left.

Cost: Free.

Bathrooms: Portable toilets, indoor bathroom when office is open, M-F 8am-4pm.

Best Time to Visit: Multiple special events throughout the year, animals in enclosures, barns available for visiting year round. Lot plowed in winter.

Trail Conditions: Flat, wide, mostly level, hard-packed gravel or wood chips, very easy to follow. Trails well maintained.

Distance: 0.75 mile loop trail.

Parking: Parking is a little confusing—for non-members, drive into main entrance, continue through the farm buildings, look for signs pointing to visitor parking, which is actually near the back entrance of the property (right next to the portable toilets).

Open fields offer some lovely views of this property, and one of the trails traverses a large stand of rhododendrons that were planted according to Frederick Law Olmsted's design. A quiet stream flows through the property, and a small bridge allows for an easy stream crossing.

Some nice stone walls and large glacial boulders in the woods are part of what make this an interesting walk. The farm animals (sheep, of course, plus goats, geese and more) are a popular draw for visitors.

The Sheep Pasture offers many programs for children and families. This is a very compact piece of land just across the street from Stonehill College and Main Street, North Easton Center.

Foxborough

FOXBOROUGH

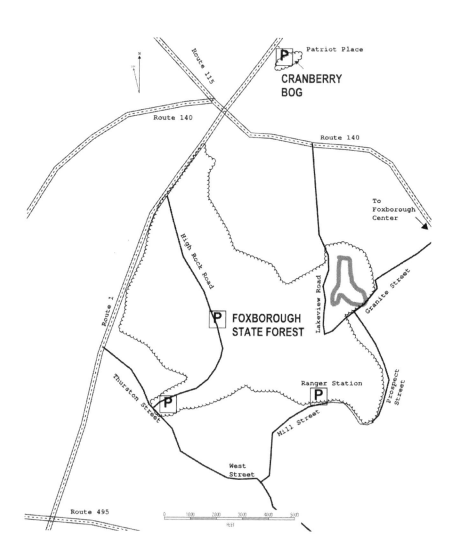

Nature Trail and Cranberry Bog at Patriot Place

Features: Cranberry bog, cranberry harvest in the fall.

Trail Map: Not available online.

GPS Coordinates: 42°05'02.02"N 71°16'24.18"W

FOXBOROUGH

Directions: Rt. 495 to Rt. 1 north, 4 miles to Patriot Place (look for the football stadium) take first light on right into parking, parking on right to side of Bass Pro Shop.

Cost: Free.

Bathrooms: Directly inside Bass Pro Shop restaurant entrance at back of building, when store is open, M-Sat. 9-9, Sun. 10-7.

Best Time to Visit: Year round, cranberry harvest in fall, lots of family events.

Trail Conditions: Sloped ramp to trail, wooden boardwalk over swamp area, dirt track along bog and loop trail. Far side of the bog trail is quite steep for a short distance.

Distance: 0.5 mile loop.

Parking: Large, packed dirt parking lot adjacent to Bass Pro Shop.

Throughout spring, summer and fall visitors are able to see workers tending the cranberry plants in the bog that is the focal point of this trail. A large cranberry festival each fall draws large numbers of visitors, who are invited to see the cranberry harvest.

The half-mile loop trail takes walkers alongside the bog, over a boardwalk, and into a small woodland area. The path is well maintained, clear, easy to follow, and offers a unique opportunity to see a working cranberry bog up close.

The cranberry bog lay abandoned for years until it was recently put back into production. The trail and reclaimed cranberry bog is a cooperative project between Bass Pro Shop,

Patriot Place and Ocean Spray, Inc. You do not have to go through Bass Pro Shop to access the trail.

It's gratifying to see several commercial entities working together to create this unique spot. The elk out in the midst of the cranberry bog add interest, but if you look closely you'll soon realize they're statues.

FOXBOROUGH

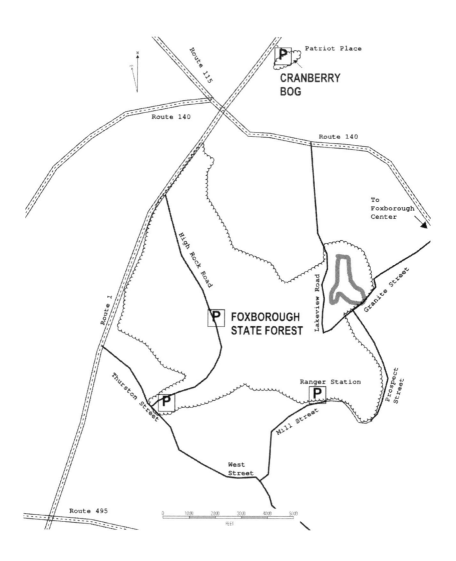

Foxborough State Forest

Features: Multiple trails, Warner Trail traverses this property. Small streams, pond, large boulders. Hunting permitted during hunting season, ATVs (All-Terrain Vehicles) permitted in warmer months.

Trail Map: Online search—Foxborough State Forest

GPS Coordinates: 42°02"54.56"N 71°16'13.93"W

FOXBOROUGH

Directions: 45 Mill Street (Ranger Station) Rt.495 to Rt. 1 north. Take a right at light onto Thurston Street, which becomes West Street. Pass Normandy Farms Campground, then take left onto Mill Street, Ranger station is on the left.

Cost: Free.

Bathrooms: Yes.

Best Time to Visit: Year round. Use care during hunting season—wear blaze orange.

Trail Conditions: Well marked wide dirt track. ATVs allowed (not in winter).

Distance: 23 miles of trails, many shorter loop trails available on this 1,027 acre property. "Heart-healthy" marked trail is an easy walk.

Parking: Behind ranger station off Mill Street, overflow lot across the street from the ranger station. Parking lot plowed in winter.

Foxborough State Forest (F. Gilbert Hills State Forest) is heavily used and has a ranger's station on the property. The trails in this state forest are in good shape, and many are quite wide and well-marked. The terrain is varied, with lots of gently sloping paths through this extensive trail system. At least one "heart healthy" trail is marked on the trail map.

A medium-sized pond (shown on the trail map) is quite pretty, but we found the trail to the pond was poorly marked. At least one road traverses the forest; beware of cars while hiking.

FOXBOROUGH

This property is quite popular with dog walkers. Signs at the entrance to the trails near the ranger station on Mill Street warn of hunting season and note times when ATVs are forbidden on the trails. Wearing blaze orange is essential during hunting season.

Framingham

FRAMINGHAM

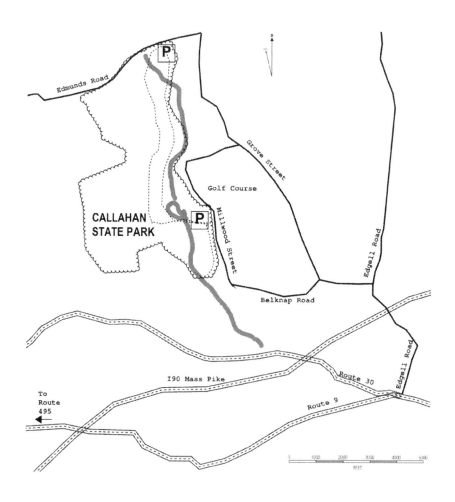

Callahan State Park

Features: Broad open trails, well marked, very dog-friendly.

Trail Map: Online search—Callahan State Park

GPS Coordinates: 42°19'15.20"N 71°27'49.51"W

Directions: Millwood Street, Framingham. Rt. 9 west to Rt. 30 exit, take right (northbound) at first set of lights to Edgell Road, left onto Belknap Road, right onto Millwood Street. Entrance on left across from golf course.

Cost: No.

Bathrooms: Portable toilets in warmer months.

Best Time to Visit: Year round.

Trail Conditions: Clear, unimproved dirt track, marked trails, a few rocks and roots, relatively level.

Distance: 7 miles of trails.

Parking: Large parking area off Millwood Street, additional parking off Edmonds Road. Lot plowed in winter.

This 820-acre property is a state park. The south section next to Millwood Street is extremely popular with dog walkers. We found what we thought was a dog-training class, which turned out to be a group of off-leash dogs, and their owners who frequent the park on a regular basis. The small pond quite near the parking area near the golf course off Millwood Street is designated as a swimming spot for dogs only. Be prepared to meet dogs on the field adjacent to the parking area and on nearby trails. Once we were just a short distance from the open field next to Millwood Street we saw few dogs on the trails.

Some trails have roots and rocks, but are relatively wide, clear, and mostly level tracks. Deer Run Trail was probably the rockiest of all the trails we walked. A stream intersects this path, and a small, 2-foot wide bridge provides solid, but narrow footing. The bridge has no railings. Following the map we downloaded, we were able to walk an easy loop trail starting from the parking lot at Millwood Street.

Along the trail we saw signs of horses and encountered mountain bikers. The dike near the Millwood Street parking makes for easy walking and offers some limited views. It is accessed immediately from the parking area.

The portion of this property accessed from Edmonds Road, which is contiguous with the rest of the state park, is overseen by the Sudbury Valley Trustees. Dogs are required to be on leashes on the Sudbury Valley Trustees portion of this property. Additional park property is north of Edmonds Street, which becomes Parmenter Street. Access is off Meadow Road, at the end of Parmenter Street.

The multiple stone walls throughout this property offer clues to the changes in land use since the 1800s.

FRAMINGHAM

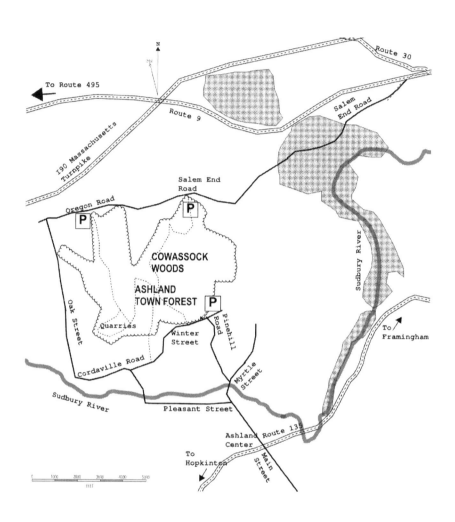

Cowassock Woods

Features: Overseen by Sudbury Valley Trustees. Adjacent to Ashland Town Forest. Multiple stone walls, land settled by refugees from Salem witch trials.

Trail Map: Online search—Cowassock Woods

GPS Coordinates: 42°17'09.94"N 71°28'18.72"W

FRAMINGHAM

<u>Directions</u>: From Framingham: Driving south on Edgell Road, cross Rt. 9 and take immediate right onto High Street. Bear left, follow Salem End road about 2 miles. At 3-way intersection, take middle road, which is still Salem End Road, continue 0.8 miles to small parking area. Access is across the street from houses numbered 886 and 890.

From Ashland: Follow Main Street north from Rt. 135 0.5 miles, road bears left, becomes Pleasant Street. 0.5 miles down, the road bears right and becomes Cordaville Road. At next fork (0.5 miles) bear right onto Oak Street. Follow Oak Street 1 mile to Oregon Road, which becomes Salem's End Road when you cross over into Framingham.

<u>Cost</u>: Free.

<u>Bathrooms</u>: No.

<u>Best Time to Visit</u>: Year round.

<u>Trail Conditions</u>: Clear, unimproved track, poorly marked trails.

<u>Distance</u>: This small parcel (about 50 acres) has loop trails of about 1-2 miles, but is contiguous with Ashland Town Forest, which has an extensive trail system in its 500+ acres parcel.

<u>Parking</u>: Very small parking area across from houses marked 886 and 890, Salem End Road, Framingham.

We entered a piece of history when we visited Cowassock Woods on Salem End Road right over the line from Ashland into Framingham. The name of the road gives a hint of its story. People fleeing the Salem witch trials in the late 1600s settled this land. The history of the area prompted the naming of the street that bounds the north side of this conservation property.

Large glacial boulders are scattered throughout the property, and small brooks flow through the area. Impressive "wolf" trees alongside the trail—trees that are much larger than any of the surrounding woods—provide evidence the woodland was once open farmland.

This Sudbury Valley Trustees property is adjacent to the Ashland Town Forest and has nice easy walking paths throughout.

Holliston

HOLLISTON

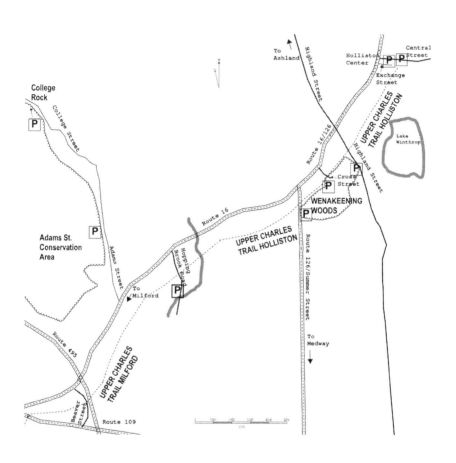

Holliston Upper Charles Trail

Features: New Year's Eve "Lantern Walk," rail-trail, connects with Milford Upper Charles Trail, stone railway bridges and tunnel.

HOLLISTON

<u>Trail Map:</u> Online search—Holliston Upper Charles Trail

<u>GPS Coordinates:</u> 42°11'59.96" N 71°25'29.81"W

<u>Directions:</u> Traveling north from Milford on Rt. 16/126, turn right at blinking light in Holliston Center onto Central Street, look for gazebo, trail head on right.

<u>Cost:</u> Free.

<u>Bathrooms:</u> No.

<u>Best Time to Visit:</u> Year round, but the trail is not plowed in winter.

<u>Trail Conditions:</u> Portions are wide, flat, packed stone dust, but some sections are very rough, unlevel track. Trail slated for improvements. When completed, the entire Holliston section of the Upper Charles Trail will be packed stone dust.

<u>Distance:</u> Approximately 5 miles till Holliston portion intersects with paved Milford section of trail.

<u>Parking:</u> Park across the street from Gazebo on Front Street or in municipal lot on Exchange Street. Additional parking available weekends at Hopping Brook industrial complex, where Hopping Brook Road intersects Rt. 16 near Milford town line. Future parking for 25 vehicles is planned at the Solect Solar Facility at 58 Hopping Brook Road, slated for construction in Summer 2015. On-street parking on Cross Street—from Holliston Center travel west on Rt. 16/126, turn left at Phillips 66 Station (Cross Street). Trail intersects Cross Street 0.1 mile. Park at the paved area on the

northeasterly side of Cross Street. Parking access is also available along the Milford section of the Upper Charles Trail; at Louisa Lake, Dilla Street; Fino Field, Main Street (Rt. 16); Friendly's, Rt. 109; and Rt. 85 near Hopkinton Town Line. (See map for Adams Street Conservations area, Holliston.)

Presently this rail-trail starts in Holliston Center and heads southwest toward Milford, MA, meeting up with the Milford Upper Charles Trail. The Milford section is complete and paved from where it connects with the Holliston section, southwest through downtown Milford, then northeast past Louisa Lake, underneath Rt. 495, currently ending at the parking area on Rt. 85 in Milford, near the Hopkinton town line.

An existing 8-arch stone bridge is planned for inclusion as part of the Trail beyond Holliston Center, north, toward Sherborn; however, this arched bridge is not easily accessible at present. The Phipps Tunnel, which travels under Highland Street, is made of granite blocks and is a highlight along the presently developed Trail. Additional stone bridges carry the Trail over local roads near Holliston Center.

The Holliston Upper Charles Trail traverses numerous neighborhoods, woodland areas, businesses, and farmland. One section intersects Army Corps of Engineers property, and offers views of wetlands and small streams. Its variety makes this section of the Upper Charles Trail a real treat to visit.

HOLLISTON

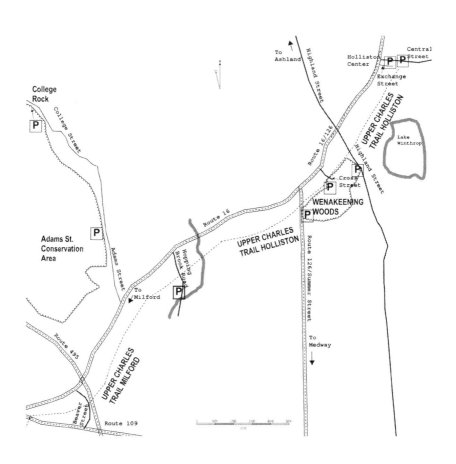

HOLLISTON

Wenakeening Woods

Features: Stone walls, small streams, wetlands.

Trail Map: Online search—Wenakeening Woods

GPS Coordinates: 42°10'55.89"N 71°25'53.02"W

Directions: Two entrances—on Summer Street (Rt. 126) almost directly across the street from Fatima Shrine in Holliston, 0.5 miles before intersection with Rt. 16; and on Highland Street—from Rt. 16/126 heading toward Holliston center, turn right at light onto Highland Street, drive about 0.5 mile; just before Medway line, look on right for trail kiosk and parking.

Cost: Free.

Bathrooms: No.

Best Time to Visit: Year round.

Trail Conditions: Clear, unimproved dirt track, trail markings, relatively level with some rocks and roots.

Distance: Loop trails, 100 acres, about 2 miles of walking trails.

Parking: For about 6 cars off Highland Street, (a sort of blocked off fire road), room for 2 cars off Summer Street (Rt. 126), almost directly across from the Fatima Shrine. Alternative access is available on Cross Street; turn off Rt. 16/126 at the Phillips 66 Station, follow Cross Street. Upper Charles Trail intersects Cross Street in 0.1 miles. Park at the paved area on the northeasterly side of Cross Street.

Wenakeening Woods was donated as open space by the Avery Dennison Corporation; one of their buildings is adjacent to this property. Access to the trail from Highland Street is through a break along the stone wall that abuts the parking area. No sign is posted in the kiosk on Highland Street to indicate that this is Wenakeening Woods; however, a large sign is visible once you've entered the woods trail.

Within the property itself there are numerous stone walls. We found a stone structure that was perhaps a well, now filled with a rather large tree. A boulder pile may have been put there as part of construction for the Avery plant, which is just visible through the woods in one portion of the property. The paths are marked and have several different loop trails, but some of the markings are confusing.

HOLLISTON

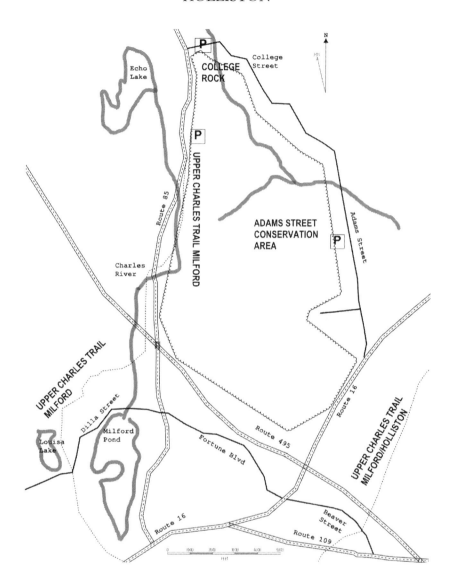

Adams Street Conservation Area

Features: Connects with additional conservation areas: New England Mountain Bikes (NEMBA) "Vietnam" property, Upper Charles Trail in Milford at Rt. 85, and College Rock, (in Hopkinton section of this book).

HOLLISTON

<u>Trail Map</u>: Online search—Holliston MA open space maps

<u>GPS Coordinates</u>: 42°10'40.14"N 71°29'00.91"W

<u>Directions</u>: Rt. 495 to Exit 19-Rt. 109 Milford. At end of ramp, head west on Rt. 109 one block to Beaver Street, turn right onto Beaver Street, go 0.5 mile to East Main Street, Rt. 16. Turn right onto Rt. 16, go under Rt. 495, follow Rt. 16 for about 1 mile to left onto Adams Street. Follow Adams Street about 1 mile to Adams Street Conservation area on left. Alternative, access trails at the Upper Charles Trail in Milford on Rt. 85 (near Hopkinton town line), or College Rock in Hopkinton.

<u>Cost</u>: Free.

<u>Bathrooms</u>: No.

<u>Best Time to Visit</u>: Year round.

<u>Trail Conditions</u>: Trails are marked. Unimproved dirt track.

<u>Distance</u>: There are miles of trails in this 2500 acre property, which is bounded by Rt. 16 in Holliston and Rt. 85 Milford/Hopkinton and Rt. 495. Small loop trails near the Adams Street entrance.

<u>Parking</u>: Space for approximately 10 cars up a sloped driveway off Adams Street. Additional parking for 30 cars from access at Milford Upper Charles Trail parking off Rt. 85 Milford, near Hopkinton town line. Very small parking area at College Rock, Hopkinton.

This large area of contiguous parcels of conservation land provides a variety of experiences for people with different interests. Easy, level trails for those looking for easy walks, and rocky, hilly terrain for those who want exciting mountain bike adventures in the area owned by the New England Mountain Biking Association (NEMBA). The NEMBA "Vietnam" property is some distance from any of the parking areas, so expect to encounter bike riders on these trails.

The paths are well-marked, clear, with lots of stone walls throughout this nearly 2500-acre property. You'll find wide as well as narrow trails, some roots and rocks, along with vernal pools and streams, but nothing to prevent an enjoyable walk.

Hopkinton

HOPKINTON

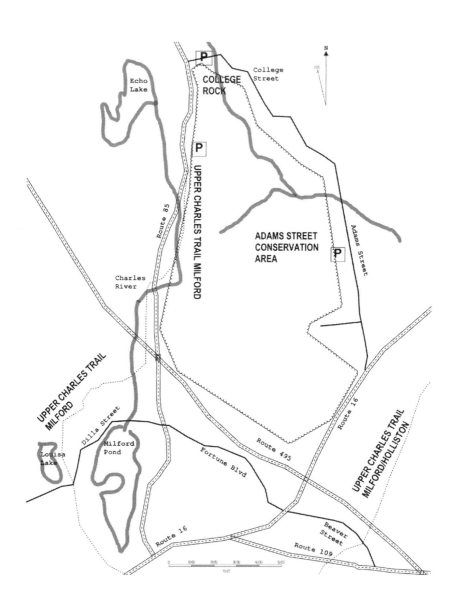

College Rock

Features: College Rock—large rock outcrop. Adjacent to Adams Street Conservation area, Holliston.

Trail Map: Online search—Trail map College Rock Hopkinton

GPS Coordinates: 42°11'42.62"N 71°29'56.34"W

Directions: Rt. 495 to Rt. 85, (Milford) head north on Rt. 85 for 2 miles toward Hopkinton Center; just after crossing into Hopkinton, look for College Street on right, turn onto College Street, go 0.2 miles, look for parking area on right.

Cost: Free.

Bathrooms: No.

Best Time to Visit: Year round, but parking lot may not be plowed in winter.

Trail Conditions: Clear paths, unimproved track, can be muddy near brook that flows next to the rock outcrop. Some rocks and tree roots in path, mostly level.

Distance: Short (0.5 mile) loop trail around College Rock, additional trails beyond College Rock in adjacent Adams Street Conservation Area properties.

Parking: Space for about 5 cars in hard-packed dirt parking area directly off College Street.

The path that immediately encircles the large rock outcropping is open, well-worn and mostly level. While the rock face of College Rock is impressive, the approach from the opposite side of the rock gently slopes upward toward the top of the rock, making it an easy climb and a fun area to explore. Be watchful of young ones who might be unaware of the steep drop-off on the edge of the rock face.

HOPKINTON

From this area trails lead directly toward the Adams Street Conservation area. The blazes heading toward Adams Street area are worn, but the tracks are clear, well-worn, with some rocks, and mostly level.

HOPKINTON

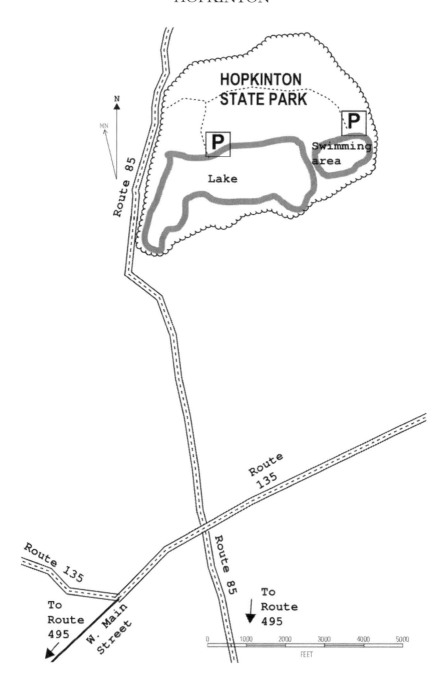

Hopkinton State Park

Features: Large pond with a spillway, popular picnicking area, extensive trails, seasonal boat rentals.

Trail Map: At kiosk at entrance to park; online search—Hopkinton State Park trail map

GPS Coordinates: 42°15'41.89"N 71°31'27.61"W

HOPKINTON

Directions: 164 Cedar Street (Rt. 85) Hopkinton. Rt. 495 to Rt. 85 north, cross Rt. 135 in Hopkinton Center, continue on Rt. 85 for 2.4 miles, look for large pond on right, state park signs.

Cost: $8 seasonally—pay at entry kiosk; no charge in winter months.

Bathrooms: When park is open.

Best Time to Visit: 8am-8pm year round—boat rentals in summer, more limited parking in winter. Caution: hunting permitted during hunting season—wear blaze orange.

Trail Conditions: Unimproved, broad, dirt track, trails well-marked. Some inclines along trails.

Distance: 1.5 mile "Heart Healthy" loop trail, additional trails throughout park.

Parking: There are extensive parking areas throughout the park during the summer season, but much of the parking is gated off in the winter. Paved access to parking near the boat rental area is plowed and open year round.

This is a very popular spot for dog walkers. It is also seasonally an extremely popular spot for swimming, sailing and kayaking. The boat rental concession at the lake is quite busy throughout the spring, summer and fall months. Look for good deals on used boats in the spring.

A designated "heart healthy" loop trail follows the north shore of the lake near the boat rental area. The paths are somewhat rocky, somewhat hilly in some sections, clear and well-maintained.

A large dam structure created the lake at this popular state park, but on a visit in the fall, the water was so low that the lower lake area was almost totally dry. This gave us a chance to see the dam spillway structure, made of carefully cut stone blocks, which drops down like a stairway away from the dam. A very similar structure is found in the spillway at the Ashland Reservoir, but Hopkinton's is much larger.

Large-group events take place regularly at this state park. Check the DCR website for details on renting picnic areas.

HOPKINTON

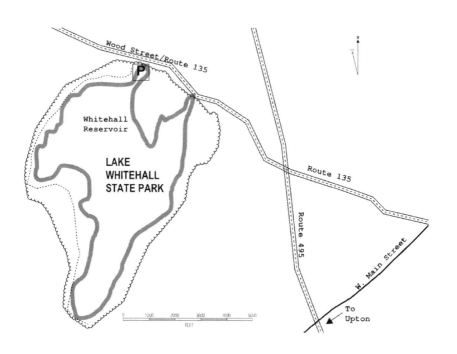

HOPKINTON

Lake Whitehall State Park

Features: Primarily for motor boating—boat ramp and designated parking on Rt. 135 almost exclusively for boats with boat trailers or cars with racks for kayaks and canoes.

Trail Map: Online search—Lake Whitehall State Park

GPS Coordinates: 42°14'29.85"N 71°34'22.42"W

Directions: From Hopkinton Center, head west on Rt. 135 to Rt. 135 (Wood Street) and W. Main Street intersection. Bear right to stay on Rt. 135 (Wood Street), north 2.5 miles toward Westborough, parking is on left on Wood Street. Trail head starts at Wood Street.

Cost: Free.

Bathrooms: Portable toilets placed seasonally, not in winter.

Best Time to Visit: For hiking, off-season (early spring, fall, winter).

Trail Conditions: Rough, mostly level, unimproved track roughly follows the north shore of the reservoir. On the south side of lake, the trail encounters some private property. The north trail is much easier going.

Distance: About 6.5 miles around the pond, but access to parts of the south side of the shoreline is blocked by private property. Three miles to the far side of lake starting from Wood St.

Parking: Space for about 50 cars (with trailers). Very limited parking for cars with no trailers. If hiking, drive as though approaching boat ramp, go just beyond ramp, park on edge of parking lot. Additional parking on Winter, Spring, and Pond Streets. The Wood Street lot is plowed in winter.

Do not expect a quiet retreat in the summer at the height of Lake Whitehall's summer boating activities. A well-known and well used boating spot in central Massachusetts, this lake's large parking lot is indicative of how many people visit here.

Houses are not visible along the shore, so when visiting "off season," it has the feel of a quiet get-away. When we visited in the late fall, we met only one other person along the trail. We found easier walking on the north side of the pond starting from the Wood Street parking lot and easily followed the blue-blazed trail along the north shoreline. The path travels alongside the shoreline and is clear, well-maintained, with nice views of the water along the entire path.

We did not attempt to circumnavigate the entire pond--over 6 miles of trail if you are ambitious. The trail to the south of the boat ramp is rather rooty, extremely sloped in sections, and has some rocks.

HOPKINTON

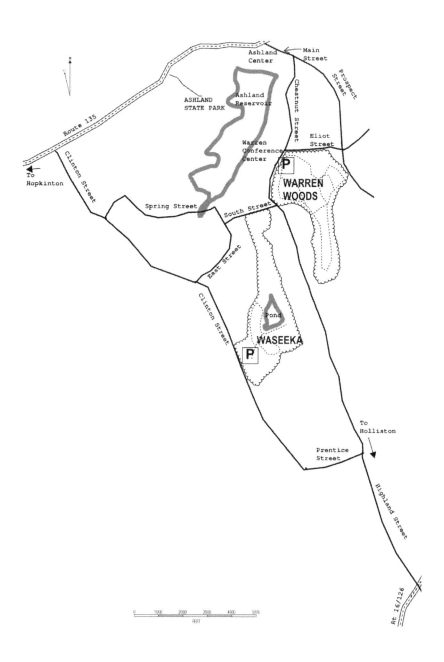

Waseeka Wildlife Sanctuary

Features: Pond, beaver activity, evidence of past forest fire.

Trail Map: Online search—Waseeka Mass Audubon Trail map

GPS Coordinates: 42°12'59.04"N 71°27'52.18"W

Directions: From the intersection of Rt. 85 and Rt.135 in Hopkinton center, head east toward Ashland on Rt. 135 for 2 miles, turn right onto Clinton Street, travel almost exactly 2.1 miles. Parking on left.

Cost: Free.

Bathrooms: No.

Best Time to Visit: Year round.

Trail Conditions: Clear, broad, mostly level, unimproved dirt track, well marked.

Distance: 1-mile loop trail, additional smaller loop trail, 229 acres.

Parking: Space for 6 to 8 cars in well-marked parking area visible from Clinton Street.

Beaver activity and subsequent flooding has caused the rerouting of the trail system at this Mass Audubon property, which is overseen by Mass Audubon Broadmoor in Natick. The trail ends at the far side of the dike that originally created the pond.

On two sections of the loop trail near the pond, we saw clear signs of past forest fires: charcoal and black markings on stumps and up the side of trees were evident. The fire, which appears to have covered several acres of the property, cleared the underbrush of white pines. There are noticeable differences between these areas and the sections that had not been burned. Numerous white pine saplings fill the understory that was untouched by fire.

We saw fresh wood chips from beaver chews quite near the shore of the pond—the path the beaver used to access the pond was quite clear and well used. We did not spot any beavers on our visits, sadly, but they are (as their reputation promises) very busy maintaining their dam at the east side of the pond. A nice, quiet spot with several short, interesting loop trails within this small property.

HOPKINTON

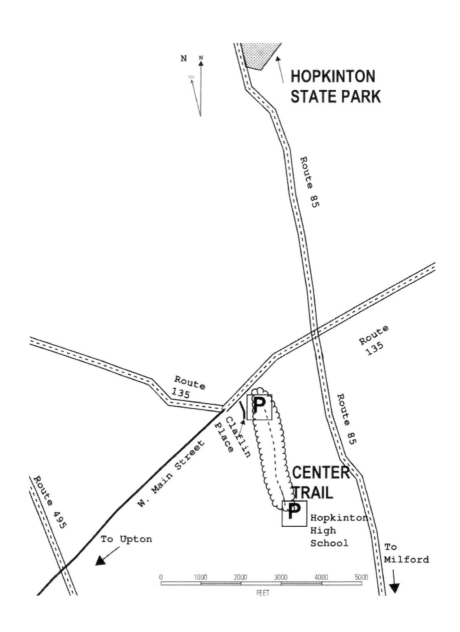

Hopkinton Center Trail

Features: Crushed stone rail-trail. Planned for inclusion in Upper Charles Bikeway.

Trail Map: Search online—Hopkinton Center Trail map

GPS Coordinates: 42°13'31.10"N 71°31'45.72"W

Directions: Parking at Hopkinton High School and Hopkinton Middle School (Rt. 85) with additional small amount of parking immediately off Rt. 135, directly across from Hopkinton Lumber at Claflin Place near downtown Hopkinton.

Cost: Free.

Bathrooms: No.

Best Time to Visit: Year round.

Trail Conditions: Packed stone dust, wide (8-10 ft) rail-trail.

Distance: 0.6 mile from Hopkinton Center to Hopkinton High School where trail presently ends.

Parking: Small dirt parking area adjacent to trail just off Claflin Street, additional parking at back of Hopkinton High School.

This section of rail-trail is a work in progress. Planned as part of the Upper Charles Trail, it is presently accessible only from behind Hopkinton High School, and from parking just off Rt. 135 on Claflin Place. Further land acquisitions are in process, but this rail-trail is not yet connected with the Milford section of the Upper Charles Trail.

The part of the trail that is finished is broad, level, packed stone dust that makes for easy walking and biking. Starting at Rt. 135 and headed south, the trail abuts a number of backyards, then heads through woodland before reaching Hopkinton High School.

Mansfield

MANSFIELD

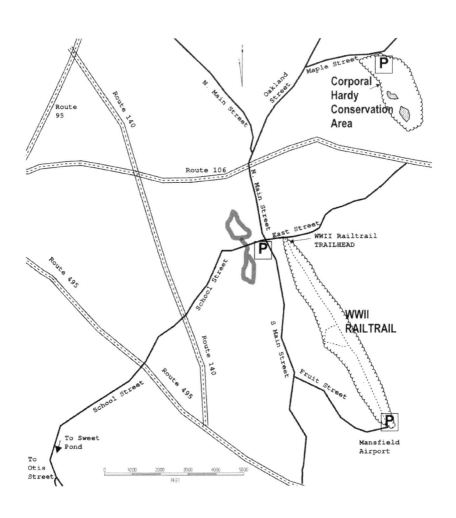

Corporal Hardy Conservation Property

Features: Formerly Maple Street Conservation area, small pond.

Trail Map: At trail kiosk; online search—Mansfield Corporal Hardy trail map

GPS Coordinates: 42° 02'35.80"N 71°12'03.66"W

Directions: Rt. 95 to Rt. 140 Mansfield-Foxboro exit, take Rt. 140 south toward Mansfield for .75 mile to left onto Rt. 106. Go another 0.75 to left onto N. Main Street. Immediately fork right onto Oakland Street, drive 0.75 miles to Maple Street on the right, travel 0.5 mile; trail kiosk and parking are on the right.

Cost: Free.

Bathrooms: No.

Best Time to Visit: Year round.

Trail Conditions: Rough, wide, unimproved track. Some trail markings. Mostly level with some inclines around pond area closest to trail head.

Distance: About a 1-mile loop trail.

Parking: Very small pull-off (1-2 cars) next to trail kiosk.

The map of this property promised two small, unnamed ponds, both of which we found. The shores of only one pond was accessible, but the trails around both ponds were clear and easily navigable. The smaller pond is filling in with vegetation and barely visible.

Trails were marked clearly, but we felt some confusion about yellow and orange—blaze colors on the map did not correspond well with what we found along the trail. We had mostly level walking to the farther pond. The path that circled the pond closer to the trail head offered some easy ups and downs that will be entertaining for younger ones while still being easily navigable.

MANSFIELD

The larger pond offered some nice spots to sit and enjoy the view from the shore. A quiet spot just outside Mansfield center, easily accessed from many neighborhoods near downtown Mansfield.

MANSFIELD

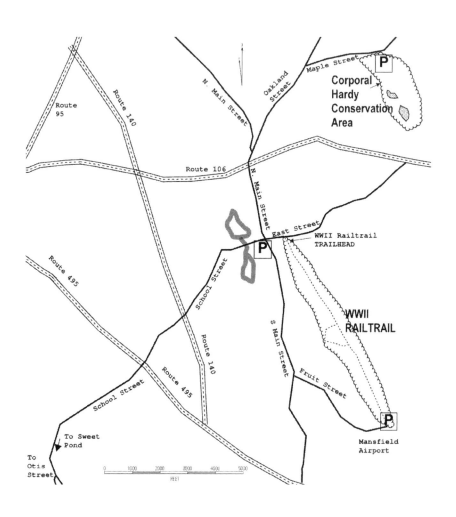

WWII Memorial Rail-Trail

Features: Bikeable paved rail-trail with additional woodland trails accessed directly from mid-point of the trail.

Trail Map: Online search—Masstrails.com Mansfield map

GPS Coordinates: 42°01'29.80" N 71°12'51.60"W

Directions: Take Rt. 95 to Rt. 140, Mansfield-Foxboro exit, then take Rt. 140 south toward Mansfield for .75 mile to left onto Rt. 106. Go another 0.75 mile to right onto North Main Street. Drive 0.5 mile to Mansfield town common, on street or municipal parking. From Mansfield town common, (S. Main Street and East Street) walk a short block east on East Street to the downtown trailhead. Alternatively:

Trailhead near Mansfield Airport: Rt. 495 south to Mansfield/Norton exit, take left onto S. Main Street (toward Mansfield Center), take first right onto Fruit Street. Follow Fruit Street past Mansfield Airport on right; trailhead is on the left just past the airport.

Cost: None.

Bathrooms: No.

Best Time to Visit: Trail not plowed in winter, but downtown Mansfield municipal parking allows access year round.

Trail Conditions: Paved rail-trail.

Distance: 1.5 miles wide, paved rail-trail from Mansfield Center to Mansfield Airport.

Parking: On-street parking available next to Mansfield Town Common or at downtown Mansfield municipal lot just off N. Main Street. Parking for about 5 cars across the street from Mansfield Airport.

Downtown Mansfield displays numerous bike-trail and bike crossing signs indicating the rail-trail that starts in the downtown. A short paved trail, this path also offers an additional woodland trail at the mid-point of the rail-trail, only accessible from the rail-trail itself. The path is well maintained, with a kiosk showing a map of the trail.

While this is a very short trail, it is heavily used by residents, dog walkers, and some bikers. Plans to connect the trail with additional rights of way through Norton appear to have been put on hold.

MANSFIELD

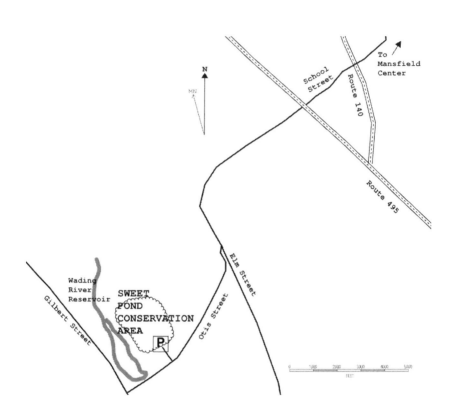

Sweet Pond

Features: Water views.

Trail Map: Online search—Mansfield Sweet Pond trail map

GPS Coordinates: 41°59'24.19"N 71°15'12.79"W

Directions: Rt. 495 to Mansfield Rt. 140 exit, travel north toward Mansfield on Rt. 140 (Commercial Street) 0.5 mile to left (west) onto School Street. Travel about 1.5 miles, Otis Street will be on your right. Turn onto Otis Street, travel 1.5 miles, look for ball fields (recreation area) on your right, turn into the road that takes you to the ball fields; trail is at edge of woods, past ball fields.

Cost: Free.

Bathrooms: Portable toilets at ball fields during athletic season.

Best Time to Visit: Year round.

Trail Conditions: Unimproved, wide, level dirt track, no trail markings, no obstructions.

Distance: A little under a mile loop trail through the woods, one portion alongside the pond.

Parking: Large parking area next to ball fields, including spots close to woods and trailhead.

This property offers a limited water view and some nice oak-pine upland. Look for the opening to the trail quite near the pond, which is actually part of the Wading River that flows just west of the parking area.

We found a few spots along the trail with views of the river, quite pretty. Look for birds and waterfowl along this section of the trail.

The loop trail is quite flat, open, and clear through a piney wood. Traffic sounds of Rt. 495 could be heard in the distance, but the walking is easy, and offers a nice spot to head to when little ones need a break from the ball game.

Medfield

MEDFIELD

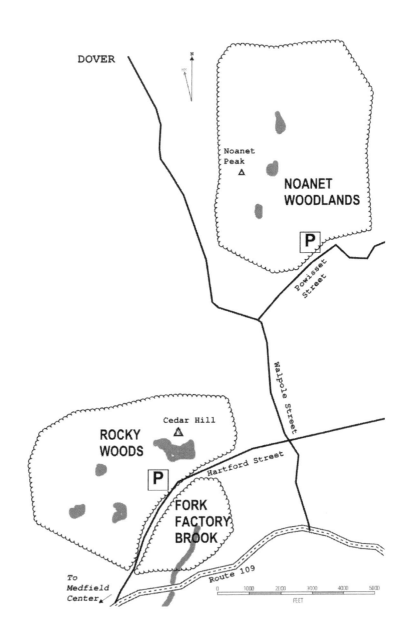

Fork Factory Brook

Features: Large rock outcropping, remnants of millrace, factory foundations.

Trail Map: Online search—The Trustees of Reservations

GPS Coordinates: 42°12'19.81"N 71°16'35.95"W

MEDFIELD

<u>Directions:</u> From Rt. 27 and Rt. 109, head east on 109 from Medfield Center for about 2 miles. Turn left on Hartford Street. Drive 0.6 mile; parking for Fork Factory Brook and Rocky Woods is on left.

<u>Cost:</u> Free for The Trustees of Reservations members and children under 12, $4 donation for non-members.

<u>Bathrooms:</u> Portable toilets at Rocky Woods.

<u>Best Time to Visit</u>: Year round, parking at Rocky Woods plowed in winter.

<u>Trail Conditions:</u> Unimproved, wide dirt track, marked trail. Mostly level paths, gentle inclines.

<u>Distance:</u> 1.5 miles of trail, not a loop.

<u>Parking:</u> Parking for 100 cars is shared with Rocky Woods, directly across the street from this property.

Park at Rocky Woods, then carefully cross Hartford Street to the Fork Factory Brook trail—traffic travels on Hartford Street at high speeds. The property has a community garden site and some large boulders along the trail. A boulder pile makes for fun climbing for the more adventurous, but no view is available from the top of the rocks.

A farm-fork (pitchfork) factory once occupied the site. We found the mill-race of the factory's mill but very little other evidence of the factory itself. Just a few feet from where we stood to examine the mill-race, cars zipped by on Rt. 109, a reminder of the modern world. We were struck by the effort undertaken to capture energy to power the mill from this small stream, and the craftsmanship that had gone into creating the stone mill-race and dam along this tiny waterway. When we visited in the fall the stream was nearly dry, so clearly this was a limited power source, subject to the change of seasons.

MEDFIELD

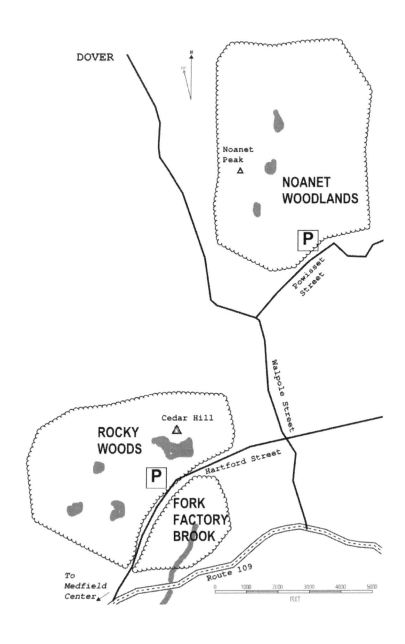

Rocky Woods

Features: Ponds, view, extensive trail system.

Trail Map: Online search—The Trustees of Reservations

GPS Coordinates: 42°12'19.81"N 71°16'35.95"W

Directions: From Rt. 27 and Rt. 109, head east on 109 from Medfield Center for about 2 miles. Turn left on Hartford Street.

Drive 0.6 mile; parking for Fork Factory Brook and Rocky Woods is on left.

Cost: Free for Trustees members, children under 12, $4 donation for non-members.

Bathrooms: Portable toilets.

Best Time to Visit: Year round—parking lot plowed in winter.

Trail Conditions: Broad, wide, open, mostly level, unimproved dirt track. Steep climb, with water bars, to view.

Distance: 6.5 miles of trails, options to walk multiple loop trails on 491 acres.

Parking: Shared parking with the Fork Factory Brook property for 100 cars.

There are numerous ponds on this property; two of the largest are Echo Pond and Chickering Pond. Trails travel alongside the edge of the shorelines of these ponds, allowing for nice water views. There are great spots along the trails for taking photos throughout different seasons.

Cedar Hill provides a nice overlook. The approach to the hill is a somewhat steep climb. The water bars offer stair-steps up the hill to the overlook, but it may be a steeper climb than some find comfortable.

Many dogs (and their people) use the trails at Rocky Woods. Dogs are allowed to be off-leash in some sections, so be prepared for a variety of dog encounters.

MEDFIELD

Rocky Woods is an extremely popular destination, especially for group events in the summer. Check the Trustees of Reservations website to make reservations for picnic pavilions.

MEDFIELD

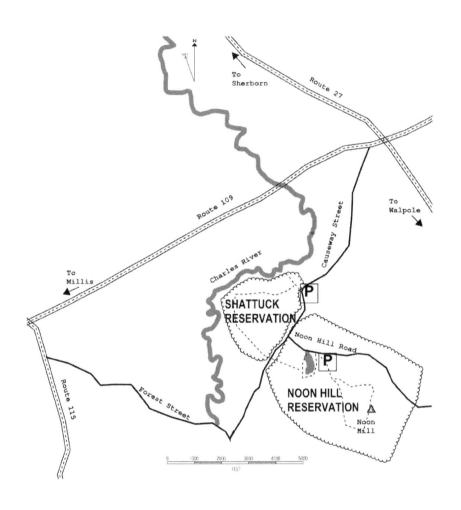

Noon Hill

Features: View, nice rock outcroppings, steep hill, small pond; Bay Circuit Trail traverses this property.

Trail Map: Online search—The Trustees of Reservations

GPS Coordinates: 42°09'52.94"N 71°19'07.97"W

MEDFIELD

Directions: From intersection of Rt. 27 and Rt. 109 in Medfield Center, head west toward Millis on Rt. 109. Travel 0.1 mile, turn left onto Causeway Street. Drive 1.3 miles on Causeway, then left onto Noon Hill Road. Parking on right.

Cost: Free.

Bathrooms: No.

Best Time to Visit: Year round—parking lot plowed in winter.

Trail Conditions: Wide, open, unimproved track, mostly level except when climbing to the view at Noon Hill. Some wet areas.

Distance: 4.5 miles of trails, loop options for shorter hikes.

Parking: On Noon Hill Road, for 15 cars on right, next to trail kiosk.

While some of the paths on this property are wet, there are small bog bridges that make the trip more pleasant. For the most part the trails are broad, clear, and well-marked, with lots of stone walls throughout the property. One of the trails was clearly a cart path in the past; stone walls line both sides of the wide, level trail.

The 370-foot summit of Noon Hill has two approaches, from the north and the south of the hill. From the trailhead on Noon Hill road, the north approach is marked with signs pointing to the summit. This approach is steeper than the second approach, on the south side of the hill. Continue on the main trail past the first, more northerly approach, follow the map and take the approach from the south for an easier climb.

Immediately to the west of the parking area is a small pond with a trail that follows the shoreline. A small waterfall flows from the dam that created the pond and offers some attractive views. Access to trails to Shattuck Reservation is from this section of Noon Hill.

MEDFIELD

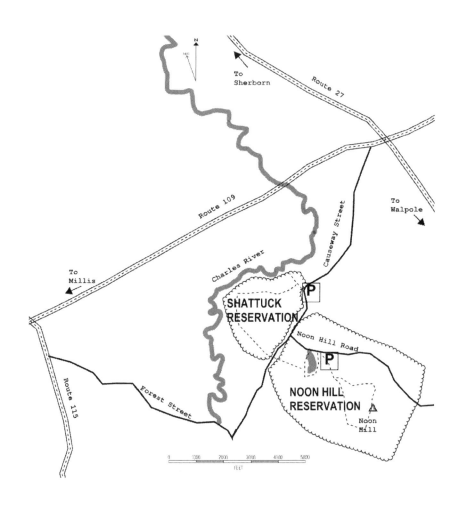

MEDFIELD

Shattuck Reservation

Features: Trail connects to Noon Hill property, portion of Bay Circuit Trail, view of Charles River.

Trail Map: Online search—The Trustees of Reservations

GPS Coordinates: 42°09'52.94"N 71°19'07.97"W

MEDFIELD

Directions: At intersection of Rt. 27 and Rt. 109 in Medfield Center, head west toward Millis on Rt. 109; travel 0.1 mile, turn left onto Causeway Street. Drive 1.3 miles on Causeway, left onto Noon Hill Road.

Cost: Free.

Bathrooms: No.

Best Time to Visit: Year round. Parking at Noon Hill plowed in winter.

Trail Conditions: Rough, narrow, mostly level dirt track, a few trail markings.

Distance: 1.5-mile loop trail.

Parking: Parking for 15 cars shared with Noon Hill property; additional very small pull-off directly on Causeway Street, 1.1 miles from Rt. 27 on the right.

This property, owned by the Trustees of Reservations, has connecting trails to Noon Hill, another property of The Trustees of Reservations adjacent to it. We found bog bridges in good repair, interesting glacial boulders and some stone walls. The ground is mostly level, and the track is clear. Some of the trail markers along the way are somewhat confusing.

We accessed the trail from a small pull-off spot on Causeway Street. A small trail kiosk is posted next to what appears to have been a small road at some time in the past. When we walked to the end of the road we got a glimpse of the Charles River.

We saw lots of ferns, were grateful for the bog bridges through some wet areas, and saw boulders and stone walls in the area. Since we visited in August we even enjoyed a few blackberries along the trail.

The Bay Circuit Trail traces a line from the North Shore, around Boston, down to the South Shore and travels through this property.

Natick

NATICK

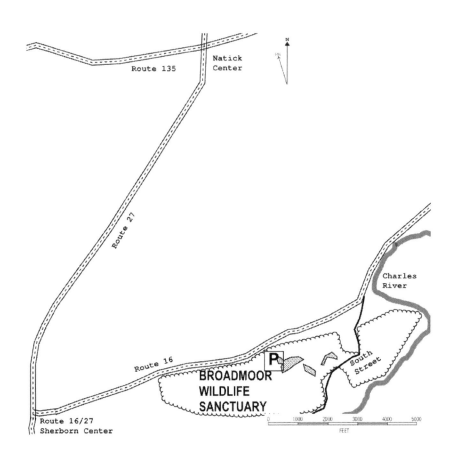

NATICK

Broadmoor Wildlife Sanctuary

Features: Closed Mondays. Access to Charles River, handicapped accessible path to boardwalk from visitor center.

Trail Map: At visitor center; online search—Mass Audubon Broadmoor Trail map

GPS Coordinates: 42°15'23.07"N 71°20'23.26"W

NATICK

<u>Directions</u>: 280 Eliot Street (Rt. 16) Natick. From Sherborn Center, Rt. 27/16, Rt. 27 continues north. Turn right at light to stay on Rt. 16, drive 1.6 miles toward S. Natick, look for sanctuary signs on right shortly after entering Natick.

<u>Cost</u>: Free for Mass Audubon members, $5 for non-members.

<u>Bathrooms</u>: Yes, when office is open, T-F 9am-5pm, Sat. and Sunday, 10am-5pm.

<u>Best Time to Visit</u>: Year round, parking lot plowed in winter, closed Mondays.

<u>Trail Conditions</u>: Handicapped-accessible trail next to visitor's center, rougher track farther from the visitor's center; dirt, unimproved track is rocky and rooty, with some inclines.

<u>Distance</u>: 9 miles of trails, 0.25 miles of handicapped accessible trail on 624 acres.

<u>Parking</u>: Substantial (30-car) parking lot next to visitor center. Space for school buses to discharge passengers.

Broadmoor (and some other Mass Audubon Sanctuaries we've visited) has a helpful blaze system—yellow blazes on trees bring you back to the visitor's center and blue blazes take you out onto the trails, away from the visitor's center.

Varied terrain awaits. We found open fields, swampy areas, small waterfalls created by dammed ponds, lots of boulders, and bare bedrock. We encountered a large beaver dam and signs of beaver in the woods, with multiple trees chewed partway or all the way through.

A very popular spot; numerous school groups make use of this area on weekdays, but they tend to stay near the boardwalk area around the pond near the visitor center and adjacent trails. Once past this area, there are lots of options for quiet trails.

A small road, South Street, intersects the sanctuary and the remainder of Broadmoor's property, which borders the banks of the Charles River. Beware of traffic—it's not a busy road, but it is a public way, so be alert. The Charles River is a short, somewhat steep walk through the woods down to the river, a very pretty spot. A loop trail follows the banks of the Charles then heads back toward the road.

Norfolk

NORFOLK

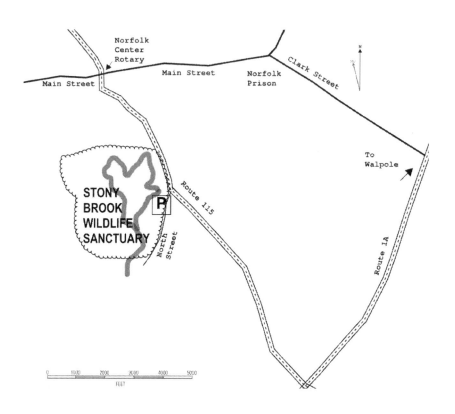

Stony Brook Wildlife Sanctuary

Features: Handicapped accessible trail, one section designed for sight-impaired. Boardwalk over swamp, dam, and waterfall.

Trail Map: Online search—Mass Audubon Stony Brook trails

GPS Coordinates: 42°06'28.18"N 71°19'02.70"W

NORFOLK

Directions: 108 North Street. From Norfolk Center, head south on Rt. 115 toward Wrentham. After about 1 mile, North Street intersects Rt. 115. Turn right, Stony Brook is immediately on your right.

Cost: Free for Mass Audubon members, $4 for non members, $3 children and seniors.

Bathrooms: When visitor center is open: Tues.-Sat. 10am-4pm, Sun. 12:30-4pm; July-August Mon. 10am-4pm

Best Time to Visit: Open year round, closed on Mondays during school year.

Trail Conditions: Handicapped accessible trail for the blind near visitor center (crushed stone), but no disabled handrails. Grade is somewhat steeply sloped in spots, very manageable for baby strollers. Wide, packed dirt track.

Distance: 2 miles of loop trail on 98 acres, with additional 140 acre of adjacent Bristol-Blake reservation. Universally accessible trail is 2000 ft long.

Parking: Paved parking area for 20 cars next to visitor center, directly off North Street. Lot is plowed in winter.

Mass Audubon's Stony Brook Wildlife Sanctuary has a long tradition of welcoming people of all ages and abilities. Their handicapped accessible trail adjacent to the visitor's center was tested by the population it was designed to serve and has won awards for its design. The loop trail through the wildlife sanctuary is handicapped-accessible for the blind for the first 2000 feet, and the rest of the loop trail has ramps that make for easy walking for parents with strollers. The boardwalk is a popular destination that offers great views, lots of birds in the area, turtles, frogs, water snakes and more. The geese are fond of the area near the visitor's center—watch your step!

The summer day camp is a popular destination for area children. Photographers often visit to catch the light over the water of the pond. The small island at the end of the boardwalk offers an opportunity to explore, surrounded by water and wildlife.

This small sanctuary packs a lot of charm into a small area, a truly lovely spot with loads of programming for families and adults. The Stony Brook Fair takes place each September and is a great introduction to what the sanctuary has to offer.

Sharon

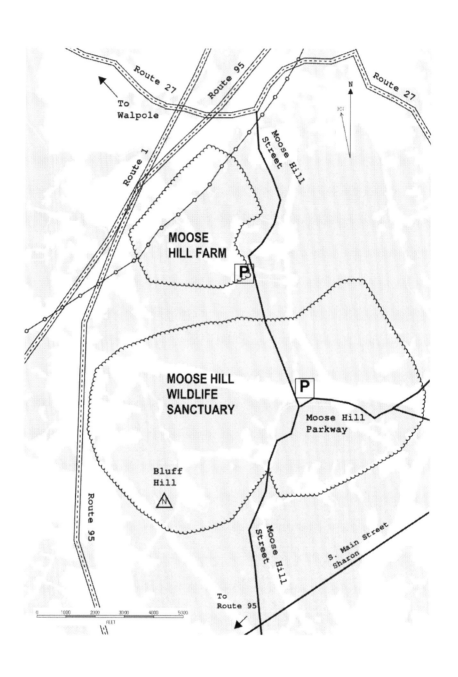

Moose Hill Wildlife Sanctuary

Features: View, stone walls, portion of Bay Circuit Trail. Oldest Mass Audubon Sanctuary.

Trail Map: At visitor's center; online search—Mass Audubon Moose Hill

GPS Coordinates: 42°07'25.35"N 71°12'28.56"W

SHARON

Directions: Intersection of Rt. 1 and Rt. 27 in Walpole, head toward Sharon on Rt. 27 (if heading north on Rt. 1, turn right onto Rt. 27, High Plain Street). First right on Rt. 27 is Moose Hill Street, follow road 1 mile, road bends sharply at Moose Hill Farm. Continue past Moose Hill Farm 0.25 mile, Moose Hill Audubon is on the left.

Cost: Free for Mass Audubon members, $5 for non-members.

Bathrooms: When visitor center is open: M-F 9-5, Sat., Sun. 10-4.

Best Time to Visit: Open year round, parking lot plowed in winter. Closed Mondays.

Trail Conditions: Rough, unimproved dirt track. Wide, mostly level paths get narrower, and steep as you approach bluff view.

Distance: 25 miles of trails, but many shorter loops possible in 1,971-acre sanctuary.

Parking: Large paved parking lot (for 50 cars) behind visitor's center, accessed from Moose Hill Parkway, adjacent to visitor center.

This Mass Audubon Property is just down the road from Moose Hill Farm, a Trustees of Reservation Property. Moose Hill Wildlife Sanctuary has many choices of trails for a variety of hiking experiences. A boardwalk traverses a swampy area; small, open fields offer great opportunities for bird watching; wide cart paths are lined with stone walls; and the effort to make the rather steep climb along the Bluff Trail results in the reward of a view from a rocky outcrop at the top of the Bluff Trail.

The view at the top of the bluff trail is to the west, overlooking the football stadium in Foxborough. The rocky outcrop offers wonderful examples of how trees thrive even in difficult environments—stunted trees survive at the top of this windblown spot, branches growing away from the prevailing wind.

The list of programs available for all ages at this Audubon sanctuary is impressive, featuring maple-sugaring demonstrations in the early spring, bird walks, plant identification classes, school vacation programs, and more. Check the Mass Audubon website for group outings, and hikes of all types.

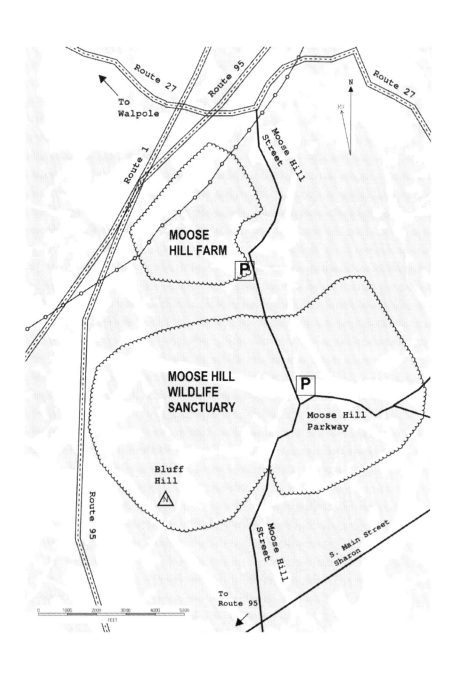

Moose Hill Farm

Features: View, old foundations, stone walls.

Trail Map: Online search—The Trustees of Reservations.

GPS Coordinates: 42°07'38.74"N 71°12'34.19"W.

SHARON

<u>Directions:</u> Intersection of Rt. 1 and Rt. 27 in Walpole, head toward Sharon on Rt. 27 High Plain Street (heading north on Rt. 1, turn right toward Sharon onto Rt.27). First right on Rt. 27 is Moose Hill Street. Follow road 1 mile, Moose Hill Farm is on the right immediately after sharp bend in road.

<u>Cost:</u> Free for Trustees members, children under 12, $4 for non-members.

<u>Bathrooms:</u> When offices are open, M-F 9am-5pm.

<u>Best Time to Visit:</u> Open year round, parking lot plowed in winter.

<u>Trail Conditions:</u> Wide, unimproved dirt track, gentle slopes.

<u>Distance:</u> 3.5 miles of trails, loop trail is shorter, about 2 miles.

<u>Parking:</u> Paved parking for about 20 cars next to farm buildings, directly off Moose Hill Street. Lot is plowed in winter.

This lovely spot offers wide, open farm fields with a view of Boston (on a clear day) from the top of the hay field. At the top of the hay field the path leads off into the woods. The trail twice crosses the power line that intersects the property, and a portion of the trail follows the power line for a short distance.

A nice section of trail beyond the power line has old house foundations and an old cart path, which is now part of the trail system. Easements noted near the power line take the trail across private property—be mindful to stay on the trail and follow the signs.

The original farmhouse, next to the parking area, is now office space for the Trustees of Reservations and sports solar panels, bringing us from the past of stone walls and abandoned house foundations, back into the present.

We've spotted flocks of turkeys, including a tom turkey, under the old apple trees at the top of the field. The trails on this property are quite easy to follow, with gentle slopes, broad, well-maintained, well-marked, and just the right length for us to get in a good walk while not feeling overtaxed.

Sherborn

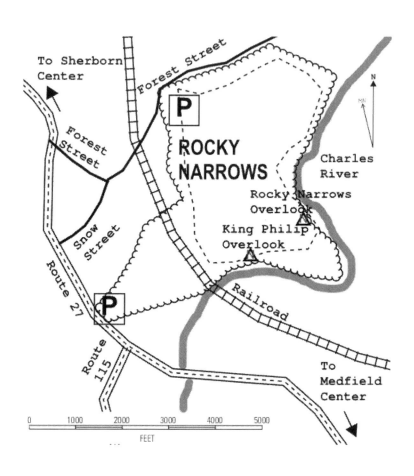

SHERBORN

Rocky Narrows

Features: Overlook views of Charles River, Bay Circuit trail traverses this property. No on-street parking permitted. Carriage road easement along banks of the Charles River.

Trail Map: Online search—The Trustees of Reservations

GPS Coordinates: 42°13'33.68"N 71°21'14.15"W

SHERBORN

Directions: From Rt. 109 and 27 in Medfield Center, head 3 miles north on Rt. 27, right onto Snow Street, 0.25 mile to Forest Street. Drive 0.5 miles on Forest Street to very small parking on right. Additional trailhead at 2.9 miles north from Medfield Center on Rt. 27, small parking area on right for access to small portion of property, limited access to remainder of Rocky Narrows, no views.

Cost: Free for The Trustees of Reservations members, $5 for non-members.

Bathrooms: No.

Best Time to Visit: Year round, parking lots plowed in winter.

Trail Conditions: Open, unimproved dirt track, wide, gently undulating trails until very steep climb to spots with a view. Some wet areas, but bog bridges in good repair.

Distance: 7 miles of trails, much shorter loop trails depending on route chosen.

Parking: 5-car limit at trailhead on Forest Street. Parking at trailhead directly off Rt. 27 for about 8 cars. No access to portion of trails with views of Charles River from parking on Rt. 27; a train line intersects this property, and crossing the tracks is prohibited.

Clear, relatively wide, well-marked trails make for easy walking on this Trustees of Reservations property. Wetlands throughout the lower elevations of this property offer lots of opportunity for bird-watching.

There are two trails that offer overlook views of the Charles River. The King Philip overlook is an easier climb than the Rocky Narrows Overlook.

An easement from Rocky Narrows follows a carriage road along the banks of the Charles for about 2 miles. Few places along the Charles River offer this kind of access. This easement in itself makes the trip to Rocky Narrows worthwhile. The views overlooking the Charles River, from the overlooks or next to the shoreline are all quite nice.

Rocky Narrows was the first Trustees of Reservations property established in Massachusetts. The biggest challenge to visiting is the lack of parking. If this property is on your list for a hike, be sure to have Plan B in your back pocket, since no on-street parking is allowed. Luckily, a number of other properties also offer easy walks very close by in Medfield, Dover, Walpole, and Millis.

Respect the two-dogs-per-person limit when visiting this property, on leash unless no other dogs are around, and always under voice control.

Walpole

WALPOLE

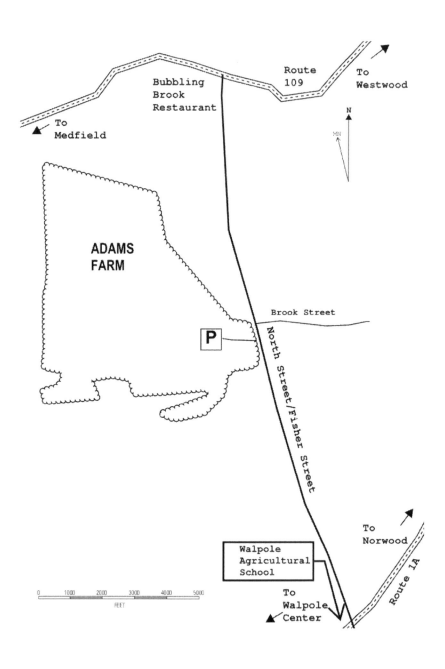

Adams Farm

Features: Bay Circuit Trail traverses property, community events ongoing, hunting not allowed. Town of Walpole property.

Trail Map: At kiosk for fee; online search—Adams Farm Walpole trail map

GPS Coordinates: 42°11'06.65"N 71°14'47.62"W

Directions: 999 North Street. From Rt. 1A and Rt. 27 in Walpole center, take Rt. 1A 1.5 miles toward Norwood, turn left just past the Norfolk Agricultural School onto Fisher Street, continue north toward Westwood, where the road becomes North Street. Adams Farm is on your left, 1 mile before Rt. 109 in Westwood.

Cost: Free.

Bathrooms: Portable toilets near trailhead.

Best Time to Visit: Year round, parking lot plowed.

Trail Conditions: Gently undulating, open carriage roads, more narrow woodland, gently sloping trails, well marked.

Distance: 10+ miles of trails, much shorter loops possible on 365 acres, additional adjoining conservation land provides total of 700 acres of conservation land available for hiking.

Parking: Packed gravel parking area for 20 cars next to red barn. Plowed in winter by Town of Walpole.

This conservation area has some woodland, some open pastures and graveled fire roads, as well as somewhat rooty and rocky paths through woodland area. The pasture trail is covered with wood chips and makes for a nice stroll through the pasture before reaching some woodland trails.

There are benches along the trail, and the paths are well-blazed. The carriage road is wide, hard-packed gravel, which allows for mountain biking through the woods.

Adams Farm has lots of events going on throughout the summer. The Friends of Adams Farm host mountain bike races, a community garden, and more. Leashed dogs are welcome, but prepare to clean up after your pet.

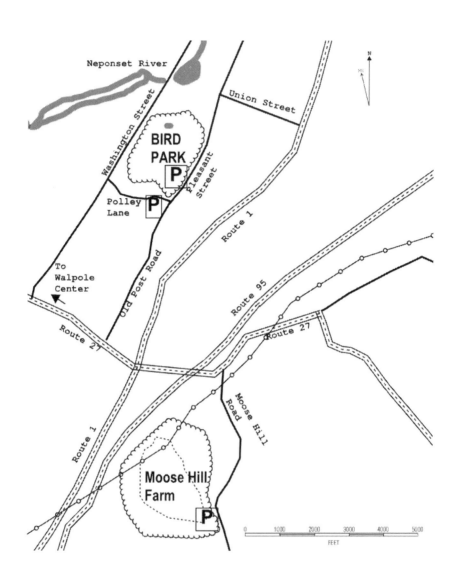

Bird Park

Features: Cement walkways, small ponds, community events.

Trail Map: Online search—The Trustees of Reservations

GPS Coordinates: 42°09'12.13"N 71°12'59.60"W

Directions: At intersection of Rt. 1 and 27 in Walpole, turn onto Rt. 27 headed toward Walpole Center. Take first right at the light to Old Post Road, drive almost 1 mile to Polley Lane, turn left, parking is immediately on the left on Polley Lane. Or continue through intersection with Polley Lane onto Pleasant Street, parking on left 0.1 mile.

Cost: Free.

Bathrooms: Available seasonally.

Best Time to Visit: Year round, many summer events. Parking lot plowed in winter.

Trail Conditions: Cement walkways in good condition, broad, open area, additional unimproved dirt tracks.

Distance: 3 miles of walking paths, many shorter loop routes.

Parking: Packed gravel parking for 60 cars on Polley Lane, additional parking for 10 cars on Pleasant Street, next to playground. Plowed in winter.

A sweet jewel of a park, 89-acre Bird Park in East Walpole is managed by The Trustees of Reservations. There are several dammed ponds in the park, part of a stream system that feeds into the Neponset River. Wide open fields are ideal for young children and families to enjoy. Paved, packed gravel or cement paths meander throughout the park, with additional dirt-packed trails tucked into the park on the section of park near Polley Lane

The playground provides a friendly place to start a visit, and sand toys are common property. Tennis courts next to the playground get regular use. One of the ponds, quite near

Washington Street in East Walpole, was at one time the town swimming pool. The dammed pond had cement walls, and area children learned how to swim at this focal point in the community. Frogs are the only thing you'll find swimming in the pond now, but if you talk to older residents they have many stories of the swimming pool at Bird Park.

Neighboring homes surround this property, which is still much used by neighbors and visitors. Numerous community events are ongoing. A real gift to the community since 1925.

Walpole Town Forest

Features: Views of Neponset River, gravel fire road.

Trail Map: Online search—Town Forest Walpole MA

GPS Coordinates: 42°07'58.79"N 71°15'11.86"W

Directions: From Rt. 27 and Rt. 1A in Walpole Center, travel on 1A headed SW toward Norfolk, turn left at the light onto

Common Street, 0.25 mile down is South Street, turn right. Follow South Street about 0.5 mile, parking on left at Neponset River.

Cost: Free.

Bathrooms: No.

Best Time to Visit: Year round, lot plowed in winter. Additional access to this trail is behind the Water Department buildings off Washington Street.

Trail Conditions: Packed dirt track, mostly level, wide, fire road.

Distance: Trail travels from South Street to Washington Street, about 0.5 mile. Not a loop. Additional town forest trails beyond Washington Street.

Parking: Hard-packed gravel for about 15 cars next to Neponset River off South Street. Plowed in winter.

Walpole offers a nice walking trail along the Neponset River, just behind Walpole High School on Common Street. A trail map is available online, but the broad, gravel fire road is relatively flat and wide, quite simple to follow to the Water Department buildings just off Washington Street. The fire road trail to Washington Street is only about 0.5 miles long, with nice views of the river, and a largish vernal pool. There are additional trails on the other side of Washington Street.

The area has several short, smaller trails that all lead back to school property. This is a heavily used property. The Neponset River bridge is particularly nice and a pretty spot to stop for a rest, or just to admire the view from a bench set nearby alongside the river.

There is a vernal pond on this property, a great spot to visit in the spring—listen for wood frogs (they sound like quacking ducks!), and spring peepers.

Westborough

WESTBOROUGH

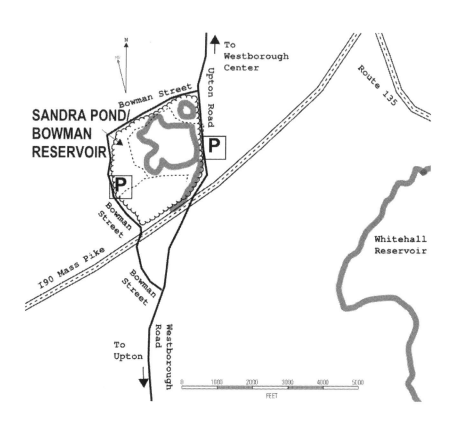

Sandra Pond, Bowman Conservation Area

Features: Water views.

Trail Map: Online search—Westborough Charm Bracelet

GPS Coordinates: 42°14'06.50"N 71°36'31.37"W

Directions: From Westborough Rotary, follow South Street (Rt. 135) south about 1 mile to right fork onto Upton Road for just over 0.9 mile to Bowman Street on the right. Follow Bowman Street 1 mile to parking on left.

Or, pass Bowman Street, continue on Upton Road 0.1 mile to Minuteman Park on right, overlooking Sandra Reservoir.

Cost: Free.

Bathrooms: No.

Best Time to Visit: Year round, difficult in winter.

Trail Conditions: Well-marked trail, unimproved dirt track, very steep in sections. Embankments near shore are quite steep.

Distance: 0.7 miles from parking on Bowman Street out to peninsula at reservoir. Additional trails surround the reservoir, but are quite steep in some sections. About 0.75 miles from Minuteman Park on Upton Road following shoreline to stairs next to Bowman Street, which are extremely steep.

Parking: Space for 4 cars on Bowman Street; for about 8 cars at Minuteman Park. Both areas hard-packed gravel.

We found the water to be quite low at Sandra Pond in the fall, not great for the reservoir, but easier for walking as we circled the banks of the pond. From Minuteman Park on Upton Street, follow the north shore of the reservoir, Sandra Pond, until you are opposite the parking area. The trails around the pond tend to follow the shoreline, so there are great water views from almost any spot along the trail.

A very steep stairway with no railings was built quite near Bowman Street, across the water and opposite the Minuteman Park. Once up this stairway, it's an easy walk along the trail to the parking off Bowman Street. Alternately, head down this stairway (from the Bowman Street parking) to follow the trail that leads back to Minuteman Park on Upton Street.

An alternative: from the Bowman Street parking, broad, level paths lead straight to the pond for some nice overlooks. Additional trails are throughout the area, but be aware that some of the trails are quite steep near the shoreline.

WESTBOROUGH

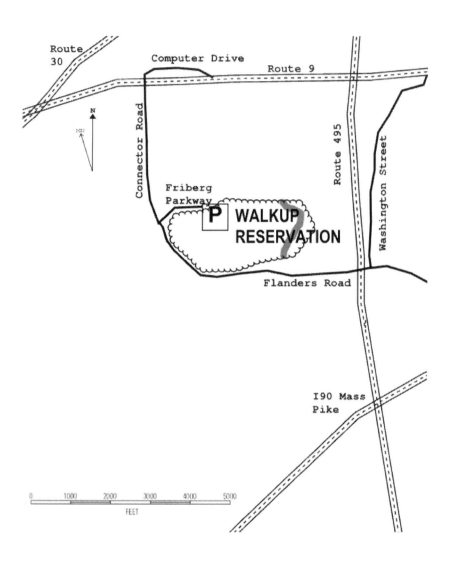

WESTBOROUGH

Walkup Reservation

Features: Surrounded by office parks, surprisingly quiet. Nice stonework, old trolley line bed, small stream.

Trail Map: Online search—Sudbury Valley Trustees Walkup Reservation map

GPS Coordinates: 42°16'48.13"N 71°34"50.68"W

WESTBOROUGH

<u>Directions</u>: Rt. 495 to Rt. 9 West, take first exit after 495, Computer Dr.; turn left at light at top of exit onto Connector Road, follow it around to drive across Rt. 9, stay straight on Connector Road about 0.5 miles to Friberg Parkway, Westborough Office Park on left. Turn left into Office Park, drive about 0.2 miles, Walkup Reservation sign on the right.

<u>Cost</u>: Free.

<u>Bathrooms</u>: No.

<u>Best Time to Visit</u>: Year round.

<u>Trail Conditions</u>: Unimproved, wide, clear dirt track. Mostly level.

<u>Distance</u>: About 1 mile loop trail, additional trails.

<u>Parking</u>: Room for about 15 cars next to Walkup Reservation sign.

Large office buildings nearly surround the Walkup Reservation, but in the middle of this property, it is surprisingly quiet. This small (63-acre) property has several mostly level loop trails to choose from and is managed by Sudbury Valley Trustees. An old trolley line intersects the property, which makes for a wide, flat path.

The property was donated to the Sudbury Valley Trustees in 1980 by Lawrence "Jack" Walkup, a lifelong Westborough resident. His family had farmed the land that constitutes the Walkup reservation for four generations, and the property is a memorial to the generations of his family who farmed there.

The small bridge that is part of the old trolley line allowed for cattle to cross from one side of the tracks to the other. We've seen this arrangement on railtrails we've visited. It's a reminder of the many changes and accommodations that were required to allow farming and commerce to coexist. The trolley line was built in 1903, and abandoned in 1931.

Parts of this property have the feel of being a wild, only slightly overgrown garden. Sculpted stone steps and stone bridges supplement the stone walls that are on the property. In all, a very scenic place. A small spot, but worth the visit.

WESTBOROUGH

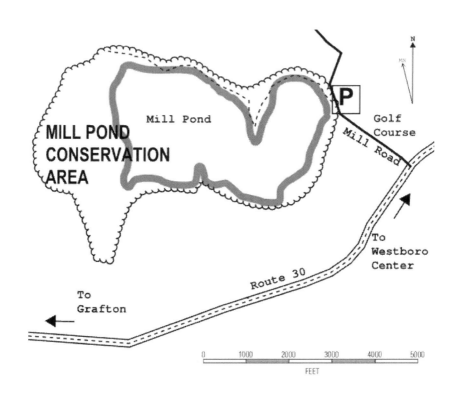

Mill Pond Trails

Features: Water views.

Trail Map: Online search—Westborough Charm Bracelet

GPS Coordinates: 42°15'57.94"N 71°38'01.30"W

Directions: Take Rt. 495 to Rt. 9 westbound, take Rt. 30 S exit, for 2.25 miles. Mill Road is on your right, just past the Westborough

Country Club on Rt. 30. Follow Mill Road 0.5 mile, look for Mill Pond on left.

Cost: Free.

Bathrooms: No.

Best Time to Visit: Year round.

Trail Conditions: Well-marked, level, dirt track, on north side of Mill Pond.

Distance: 0.75-mile walk from parking on Mill Road along north shore to train tracks and additional parking on Fisher Street. Not a loop.

Parking: Available on both sides of Mill Road, directly across from Mill Pond.

There are four trails accessible from this one parking spot on Mill Road. The trail along the north side of Mill Pond offers the easiest walking with the nicest water views. The path is clear, mostly level, with few rocks. We saw signs of beaver activity in the area.

When the leaves are off the trees you can clearly see the water almost the entire length of the mostly level path. In summer months you will want to stop at several spots along the way that offer views of the water from the shoreline.

The additional trails that lead around the golf course have some steep spots that some may find more challenging.

Resources

Websites come and go. Look for additional information by searching for the websites of the organizations that oversee properties in this area. Suggested organizations include the following:

Massachusetts Audubon Society

Charles River Land Trust

Friends of the Upper Charles

Natural Resources Trust of Easton

Natural Resources Trust of Mansfield

Sudbury Valley Trustees

The Trustees of Reservations

Bay Circuit Trail

Warner Trail

Westborough Charm Bracelet

You may also find information about area trails by searching these topics: state recreation sites, Department of Conservation

RESOURCES

and Recreation (DCR) in MA. Check town websites and look under "Conservation Department."

Look for town forests in specific towns. Some towns have extensive information about their open space.

Local Cemeteries

In addition to the trails listed in this book, consider your local cemeteries as destinations to explore. Many are paved; birds love these areas, and the neighbors are quiet!

The biggest challenge is parking—many have little parking, so take care to look for signs, educate yourself about the rules for visiting your area cemeteries, including policies about stone rubbings and picture-taking, and find out about hours when visitors are welcome. Above all, keep in mind that these are places set aside for remembrance, so be respectful while visiting.

Disclaimer: The author and contributors to this book make no representation of accuracy of content, nor guarantee rights of access to any places described herein. Users of this book indemnify and hold harmless the author and contributors.

Author's Note

First of all, thank you for reading this book. I'm always thrilled to learn that folks have used the information I've worked so hard to share. It's even nicer when I discover that this publication has encouraged families to get outside and spend time together in the outdoors.

Take a minute to write a review

If you found this book to be useful, please take the time to tell others about it. A review posted on Amazon is a real gift, whether you loved the book or have a criticism. And if you take the time to write one, you become a published writer!

Here's a little about me

As a personal and family historian, I search for and listen to the stories of people's lives. Sometimes I hear these stories in a person's living room, other times as I walk local trails I "hear" the stories of an area and "see" those who lived long before me.

My favorite stories are ones that reveal otherwise untold events in a person's life. As I explore new trails I try to work out the hidden stories of the landscape. Stone foundations appear in

AUTHOR'S NOTE

now dense woodland, a reminder that once a family (or families) made a home in what is now a quiet spot in the forest. Many of the trails we walk were once cart paths that brought goods from farms to towns over muddy, rocky, rutted tracks. Theses untold stories keep me coming back, observing, wondering, and learning.

A native Floridian, I came to New England for college, hoping to see snow. I stayed after college, and have never tired to the rocks, ponds, hill and streams (and the snow!) in this area of Massachusetts. How lucky that I am to be able to do the work that I love.

Keep in touch

If you're on Facebook, come over and "like" *Easy Walks in Massachusetts* to learn where I'm traveling to next, get a peek at updates to these books and places that will be included in future publications, and offer your thoughts about whatever you're up to in the out-of-doors. You can always get in touch by heading over to www.marjorieturner.com.

Email: Marjorie@marjorieturner.com

Made in the USA
Middletown, DE
07 June 2015